I BELIEVE IN MISSION

Other titles in the new 'I Believe' series

I Believe in Taking Action
by Steve Chalke

I Believe in the Family
by Gary Collins

I Believe in the Supremacy of Christ
by Ajith Fernando

I Believe in Mission

Alistair Brown

Hodder & Stoughton

LONDON SYDNEY AUCKLAND

First published in Great Britain 1997

1 3 5 7 9 10 8 6 4 2

British Library Cataloguing in Publication Data
A record for this book is available from the British Library

ISBN 0 340 69427 0

Typeset by Avon Dataset Ltd, Bidford-on-Avon, Warks

Printed and bound in Great Britain by
Mackays of Chatham plc, Chatham, Kent

Hodder and Stoughton
A division of Hodder Headline PLC
338 Euston Road
London NW1 3BH

Dedication

To Captain Stephen Anderson, mission teacher to me
and a whole generation by example and encouragement

Contents

Acknowledgments

Special thanks are due to fine Christians in Livingston and Aberdeen who worked with me in mission for many years, and more recently to colleagues and friends in the Baptist Missionary Society who share today's work of mission and bring much encouragement, challenge and fun into my life. I am also especially grateful to Annabel Robson of Hodder and Stoughton for her help, patience and prayer. Above all my thanks go to my children, Alistair, Rachel, Judith and Catherine, part of whose mission is to keep me sane, and to my wife Alison, without whose love and support all ministry, including this book, couldn't be done.

Editor's preface

This new series is intended to build on the widely acknowledged success of the original 'I Believe' series, of which several volumes continue to be in print. Now as then, each book sets out to tackle one of the key issues which face Christians today. The overall aim is to stimulate informed thinking and to encourage living faith by building a bridge between the ever-relevant teaching of the Bible and the complex realities of the modern world.

As we approach the new millennium, the subject of mission is high on the Church's agenda. Whatever shortcomings in the Church's life may have been highlighted by the Decade of Evangelism, there can be little doubt that raising the profile of mission has been a key benefit. But mission can all too easily remain something we talk about in theory rather than get down to in practice. I anticipate that this book will go a long way to correct this tendency. What excites me about what Alistair has written is the way his infectious enthusiasm leaps off the page and really draws the reader in to share his passion for reaching out with the good news of Jesus. He refuses to get bogged down in unnecessary details but chooses instead to focus on what really matters in this vital area: the personal commitment of all who claim to know Christ to work to make him known in our world. There is much to ponder and much to put into practice in a book which I am very pleased to be able to include in this series.

What makes it all the more remarkable is the pressure under which it has been written. Alistair agreed to take this project on soon after his appointment as General Director of the Baptist Missionary Society, hardly the most relaxing job in Christendom! I am most grateful to him – and his family – for the trouble he has taken to fit the considerable amount of work involved in writing this book alongside all his other responsibilities. I hope you will agree with me that the result is well worth the effort.

David Stone

Introduction

THE FEROCITY OF the storm blasting against windows and doors contrasted sharply with the tranquillity inside the simple wooden chapel. The dozen of us on the seaside mission team hadn't had to think long before deciding to move our evening singalong indoors. Driving rain, howling wind and early darkness enticed no-one to brave the elements.

By 9.30 we were thinking of winding the meeting up. There weren't too many out on a night like that: the usual bunch of bored but friendly teenagers and some younger children who never seemed to go home until we closed everything down. At the front our team leader was pressing home the last few points of his evangelistic appeal, a musician hovered in the background quietly tuning his guitar in readiness for the final song, and the thoughts of the rest of us were drifting towards our cocoa and some welcome rest.

The door behind our heads slammed open. An icy blast swept down the chapel. The speaker halted in mid-sentence, and every head turned to look. A man stood framed by the door, in reverse silhouette against the black of the night, probably the fiercest and most frightening figure I had ever seen. His eyes flashed, his hair was a tangled mess, his whole body drenched. Slowly he stumbled forward, staring intently from side to side. I wanted to run – all of us did – but my legs wouldn't move. Nearer, nearer he came, his eyes roaming this way and that. Halfway up the chapel he suddenly stopped, his gaze fixed on a little seven-year-old girl sound asleep in the arms of one of our team members. 'My child! My child! I thought I'd lost you,' he cried, tears now flowing down his already wet face. His arms reached out, he clutched the child tightly to his chest, and in a moment he was gone, the door left swinging to and fro in the wind.

Later, as we were clearing up, he came back to apologise for disturbing our meeting. He'd lost track of his daughter's where-abouts earlier that night. He'd searched everywhere in the ram-shackle holiday camp where they were staying. When he couldn't find her, a fear every parent suppresses had risen inside him. As darkness fell, he'd combed the beach, oblivious to the storm, searching everywhere for his missing child. He'd looked in every rock pool, every sand dune, every clump of grass. Exhaustion combined with near hypothermia in those conditions should have gripped him by then, but he wouldn't give up. He *couldn't* give up on his daughter. He'd walked the length of each side of the coast road, fearing she'd been struck by a car and was lying injured on the verge. Back to the camp, scouring every corner, looking under every shed and asking every person he met. The chapel was the only place left. Bursting into the service was the last hope of a hurting father. 'I'd lost my child,' he said, 'and I had to find her.' Finally he had.

That night I saw a living parable. It was the same as the search of a hurting heavenly Father for his lost children. They matter and he loves them. God's search is real, it's urgent, and it's not stopping until every lost child is found.

I believe in mission.

Chapter 1

The most natural thing in the world

ARMED WITH NOTHING more than faith and determination, I set off to save the down-and-outs of Edinburgh. I knew where their hostels were, and the dark closes where the poorest slept in doorways. In God's name, I'd help.

Naive but ambitious, for I'd been a Christian for only a few months, I walked through the Grassmarket, one of the oldest areas of Edinburgh, looking for some poor drunkard I could redeem. That night there was a peculiar shortage of drunkards, which was quite discouraging, really. I walked back the way I'd come, turned, scoured the street another time, and felt like a casualty doctor when no-one's had the decency to have an accident.

I was heading up the hill out of the Grassmarket when I saw the figure lying. A man had collapsed on the steps of a church. I crouched at his side. 'Are you all right?' I asked. It was a stupid question. He was unconscious, patently not all right. A trickle of blood oozed from wounds on his face. I wondered if he had other injuries. His greatest danger was probably hypothermia. It was bitterly cold, and he could die on those steps. Not that Edinburgh's finest citizens were bothering. They walked past as quickly as they could, glancing at the wretched man and this nineteen-year-old youth kneeling beside him.

I shook him, spoke to him, prayed for him. Still nothing. I needed help, but no-one stopped. No-one wanted to get involved. The tightly shut doors of the church seemed to imprison compassion, and it wasn't being allowed out to save that man.

I tried to sit him up. I pulled at his arm, but he was a dead weight, and there was no hope that I'd be able to lift him. But at last he stirred. 'Can you hear me?' I said loudly in his ear. 'You'll be okay. Don't worry.' An overpowering reek of alcohol hung around him. He was past worrying about anything.

I glanced down the road, and my heart soared. Two policemen on patrol were coming my way. They'd help. They got closer. When they were about twenty metres distant they saw me and the man lying on the church steps. They whispered quickly, and without breaking stride crossed the road and passed by on the other side. I was so shocked I couldn't bring myself to shout for them to come back.

I turned again to my semi-conscious drunk, somehow got his face off the stone steps, and hauled him into a slumped but seated position. He tried to speak, but his words were just a mumble. There wasn't a chance that he'd be able to walk. By now I'd been there for thirty minutes. I was no nearer a solution.

'Are yae needin' ony help, Jimmy?' came a voice. I looked up to see a man as rough as his voice. He was probably one of the residents of the Grassmarket's hostels, and, like many other Scots with his kind of background, reckoned everyone in the world was called Jimmy.

'I am, Jimmy,' I replied, 'for this chap's pretty far gone.'

'I'll get some o' the lads frae doon the street,' he said, and disappeared in the direction of the Grassmarket. I doubted that I'd ever see him again, but ten minutes later he was back with two other men.

With four of us, we got my incoherent companion standing, and swayed our way down the hill. We managed to give him some soup from a mobile kitchen, found an address in his pocket, and with someone's car took him there. It was his sister's home. Her horror-struck face when she saw her drunken brother lives with me still. He was on trust from a 'drying out' unit for alcoholics. That first day out was to be his last day out for a long time.

That happened a lot of years ago. I look back now, and wonder why a nineteen-year-old lad went off to walk the streets of what was then a rough area of Edinburgh looking for people to help. And I question why virtually no-one else, not even two policemen, would stop to help an unconscious man lying on the steps of a church.

The answer to my second question, of course, is that most people have quite enough to be concerned about without getting involved with those who aren't specially their responsibility. Everyone has problems. Everyone has troubles. I certainly have. My daughters are broke, my uncle's not well, my dog's gone senile, my car won't start, my bills won't stop, my in-tray's full, my out-tray's empty, my days are too long, my nights are too short, my TV picture's fuzzy, my gutters leak, my golf shots slice, my exercise regime has been stillborn, my cat has taken ownership of my chair, and my garden has revealed its secret of a disused septic tank filled with rubble and water. Who needs more problems?

Many ask that. With broken relationships, unpayable debts, failing health or an uncertain future, why take on the worries of the world as well? Why care? Why bother about anyone else?

Christians do care, though. And they do because for them the desire to help the hurting and win the lost, the desire to do mission, is the most natural thing in the world.

Like father, like son
Why Christians care has to do with three simple points of theological logic.

God loves us
The Bible tells the greatest love story of all time. It begins with a God whose nature is loving through and through. There is not a particle of God which is not love. Every thought, motive, action and goal is unadulterated love. Such love couldn't be contained. Like a volcano which cannot be held down, it had to burst out and be showered on someone. So God made people. He made them with minds, wills, personalities, emotions, abilities, creativity and other characteristics that came from God's own being. Humankind was the perfect love match for God. He took great pleasure in the people he made, and delighted to pour his love on them.

But this love story didn't run smoothly. God's love was rejected. People chose their own way and own wisdom, and deserted God. They thought independence would bring freedom. They thought indulgence would bring pleasure. Mostly all they got was bondage and misery. Worst of all, intimacy with God became estrangement from God. But alienation never became abandonment, at least not from God's side. Year after year, generation after generation, God kept reaching out to his lost partners. At times some would turn back; at times his love would be spurned again. Barriers remained.

Finally God sent his Son to tear down the barriers. Jesus died on a cross to strip humankind of its guilt. It was an immense act of love. The measure of love is what someone will sacrifice for another person. God so loved us he let his Son die so our sin could be removed. He sacrificed him to get us. That's an unfathomable but wonderful depth of caring. And, for two thousand years, Christian history is of love restored, of people knowing God again and enjoying his goodness.

God has always loved this world and still does.

God's children inherit his nature
Becoming a Christian did something profound and significant to me. It's similar to some other experiences, but it goes further and deeper.

For example, conversion didn't merely give me a new interest, one superior to all others. When I took up photography seriously it was nearly all-consuming. I went out in all weathers to take pictures. I read photography books and magazines until 'f' stops were coming out of my ears. I scoured camera shops until I knew the intricacies of each brand and model better than most of the salesmen. I banned the family from the kitchen while I blacked it out with polythene, set up my enlarger, stayed up half the night, and eventually emerged bleary-eyed with just two half-acceptable prints. For a time I virtually ate and slept photography. Christianity has been known to keep me up through the night too, but that doesn't make it my hobby. There's something about being a Christian which is bigger than that, something far more life-changing.

Nor did my conversion simply make me a believer of Christian truth. I wasn't just changed in my way of thinking, switching preferences from one set of convictions to another, like a free marketeer becoming convinced of the benefits of common owner-ship and thus abandoning capitalism for communism. Or like a royalist becoming a republican. Or like an Apple Mac user starting to believe PCs are better. All of these are radical switches of thinking. But following Christ isn't really like that. It isn't merely acquiring new ideas.

Nor is being a Christian only a matter of taking on a new loyalty. It isn't parallel to a Spurs fan deciding he'll support Chelsea or a New York Giants fan turning to the Denver Broncos. Or Tom Hanks being dumped for Tom Cruise. Or Michael Jackson being ditched for Luciano Pavarotti. Or swapping one TV soap for another. Or abandoning one brand of washing powder for a rival. Or leaving one employer for a competitor. Christianity involves new choices but it's more than an allegiance switch.

Christianity, of course, did give me a new interest, new belief and new loyalty. Those terms are not inappropriate, but they're inadequate. Conversion was much more than any of these external changes of hobby, convictions or support. It changed me on the inside. It changed my nature.

But when the time had fully come, God sent his Son, born of a woman, born under law, to redeem those under law, that we might receive the full rights of sons. Because you are sons, God sent the Spirit of his Son into our hearts, the Spirit who calls out, '*Abba*, Father.' So you are no longer a slave, but a son; and since you are a son, God has made you also an heir. (Gal. 4:4–7)

For you did not receive a spirit that makes you a slave again to fear, but you received the Spirit of sonship. And by him we cry, '*Abba*, Father.' The Spirit himself testifies with our spirit that we are God's children. (Rom. 8:15–16)

I can't understand *why* God would want me as his son. Perhaps I've done a few good deeds with my life, but he knows everything about me, including the things that I would never put on my curriculum vitae. He's aware of all the wrong things I've done and the right things I didn't do. He even knows the sins I just thought of and haven't got round to yet. But he still wants me.

I can't explain *how* he's turned me into one of his children. My genetic make-up is the same. I still have broad feet, still have scars from childhood scrapes, still can't run fast, and I'm still five feet eight inches tall and that only with an effort. And I still feel all too human. Many of my thoughts aren't spiritual. Many temptations are terrifyingly real. Many times I'm not focused on God or his work as I should be. Yet my status has been changed. Now I'm God's son. That's my position. That's my place on earth and in heaven.

Not just mine, of course. This is true of all Christians, black or white, old or young, educated or ignorant, intelligent or dull, rich or poor, male or female, strong or weak, no matter where they're from, no matter what they've done, no matter their previous religion, no matter how they came to faith. 'Yet to all who received him, to those who believed in his name, he gave the right to become children of God' (John 1:12).

There may be more questions than answers about why and how, but the amazing truth is that ordinary people who become disciples of Jesus become God's children.

God's children have God's love

There am I, sitting peacefully in my chair reading my newspaper, when one of my children creeps up behind and runs a finger through the ever-so-slightly thinner patch in my hair. Okay, through the very thin patch. 'Dad,' I'm asked, 'are you building a landing platform for miniature helicopters?' 'Don't you need sun cream on that patch?' 'Do you think the fresh air helps your brain to breathe?' Have they no mercy? Have I bred torturers? But then I remember that I teased my father just like that. At about the same age as I am now he became follicly challenged too. What was true of him has become true of me. I always knew I'd inherit from him, but hadn't realised this is how it would begin.

Likewise Christians love lost people. The logic is simple: what is true of God becomes true of his children. As God loves the lost and his children have his nature, they love the lost too. Their hearts beat in rhythm with his. Their compassion is energised by his.

Thus a passion for mission is the most natural thing in the world. It's not there because Christians are persuaded, bullied or bribed into it. In a sense it's not even taught. It's just in us, generated by the indwelling Holy Spirit. 'Therefore, if anyone is in Christ, he is a new creation; the old has gone, the new has come!' Paul writes, (2 Cor. 5:17). Yes, a new nature has come.

Everything that changes in the Christian flows from that fact.

The Holy Spirit comes to live in the Christian. He's not an ornament to be placed on a shelf and admired. He's not a toy to be switched on from time to time for amusement. He's not a spiritual ioniser to improve the environment. He is God, and he moves into the Christian's life to take over. Some things change instantly. Some are slower. But bit by bit his nature begins to dominate. Far from being an inactive passenger on our bus, the Spirit is allowed to drive what is now his bus. He determines the destination, the route, the speed, the stops along the way, and the conditions on board. Thus everything about the Christian becomes shaped by the Spirit, down to the most fundamental of characteristics. New fruit emerges in the Christian's life: love, joy, peace, patience, kindness, goodness, faithfulness, gentleness and self-control (Gal. 5:22–3). In that list is love. It includes love for the lost. It appears in God's children because God's nature is in his children. We are the missionary offspring of a missionary Father.

Hard realities

Because mission flows from a natural instinct to love, every Christian ought to be doing it. They should be telling the gospel, helping the hurting, standing with the oppressed, championing good and challenging evil. The world should be turned upside down.

But all the 'oughts' in the world don't make something into reality. All too many aren't passionate about mission. They're not longing for chances to share their faith. They're not planning their time to prioritise the needs of others. They're not disturbers of the complacency or evil of the world.

There are exceptions, of course. But often the world doesn't even notice we exist. We're not denounced, opposed or persecuted. We don't bother anyone enough to generate antagonism. The ultimate insult to Christianity in many places is that it is so easily ignored. We affect so few the majority can treat us as irrelevant.

Why? Why aren't we known for our commitment to telling others the good news we've found? Why don't we have a reputation for being the most caring people on earth? Why are we hardly raising a ripple on the surface of the world?

There are two explanations. Neither is comforting.

We don't realise who we are
One of my all-time favourite stories is about the ugly duckling. Born less than beautiful, the poor little creature went from place to place, from person to person, looking for acceptance but always finding rejection. Finally, in a critical moment of self-discovery, he realised who he really was: not an ugly duckling at all but a beautiful swan. So he stopped living the life of a lowly, despised duck and began to live as the majestic swan he was by nature.

Too many Christians live like ducks when they're really swans. God has given them a new nature, but they hardly know it. They're so conditioned by their sense of guilt or inadequacy, so ingrained in their pattern of living, and so used to living for themselves that the new life of God in them is repressed. The new life is there, but some traits of God's nature are stunted. Often what never develops properly is compassion for others and eagerness to reach the lost.

Therefore there's little excitement for or dedication to mission. The outward vision is blinded by the dazzling importance of a personal agenda. What monopolises it is my struggles, my needs, my wants. That's not healthy or right. It's not the focus God wants, and so it holds back the Spirit. 'Do not grieve the Holy Spirit of God, with whom you were sealed for the day of redemption . . . Be imitators of God, therefore, as dearly loved children' (Eph. 4:30, 5:1). To state the obvious, it's wrong to grieve the Spirit and it's right to imitate God. But not all have sorted that out.

God's Spirit brings God's life to God's children. To live differently is to act contrary to that new nature, to live as if the new birth had never happened. The new nature of God is repressed by the old nature of self. The self-orientated Christian is doing that. It's as if he doesn't know who he really is. He's been badly born into God's family.

We aren't who we think we are
I was about eight when my family first got a car. It was an Austin A34, I think, a good and reliable vehicle if not exactly sporty or image-building. It always seemed to need five minutes' notice if you wanted to go above 40 mph and overtaking was something you

did only to tractors. It had a tiny rear windscreen and awkward doors, and it lurched rather than cruised round corners. But I shouldn't criticise. We were immensely grateful to have it. I confess, however, it wasn't really our car. It belonged to my maiden aunt, a wonderful lady who desperately needed to bestow her love and generosity on someone. Thankfully we were in the firing line. She bought the car, gave my father the keys, and said, 'The car is yours to use. You can take the family out for drives.' This was in the good old days when people actually went out for the pleasure of a drive. We'd tour back roads for three hours, always looking for somewhere suitable for a picnic but rarely finding it, with my brother and me feeling sick because of the twisty roads, then go home and convince each other we'd had a wonderful time. Often we had, and that car took us many miles to many places.

There was only one qualification about the car imposed by my aunt. 'From time to time I'll need it back. There'll be somewhere I need to go, and the car will be the best way to get there. You'll need to let me have it for those times.' Well, of course she could have it. She could reclaim the car whenever she wanted. It was her car. She owned it. We had it most of the time. She took it back when she wanted. The arrangement suited everyone.

That's the deal many reckon they've struck with God. Their lives are in God's hands for most things. They'll pray, be good church members, change the majority of their bad habits, work hard and usually be kind to people. They'll be reckoned fine Christians. The only qualification is that just sometimes they'll need to reclaim their lives. There'll be a few things they want to do that are not on God's agenda and they'll need their lives back for those. And there'll be times when God wants to take their lives places they'd rather not go, and they'll have to insist he doesn't do that. So, for ninety per cent of the time they're God's with just some occasional reclaiming of their lives for themselves. That seems a reasonable balance. The arrangement should suit everyone.

It doesn't. In a deal like that God doesn't really have the lives of those people. If you can reclaim something it's because you still own it. If people still own their lives, then they don't belong to God. Becoming a Christian involves a transfer of ownership. Paul wrote, 'You are not your own; you were bought at a price' (1 Cor.

6:19–20). Jesus was tough about this matter of ownership: 'Any of you who does not give up everything he has cannot be my disciple' (Luke 14:33). That's straight. You can't be a Christian and still have the rights to your life. It's not that there are two standards – first-class Christianity for super-committed people, and ordinary 'I'll get to heaven anyway' Christianity for lesser mortals. There's only one league of discipleship. Outside it someone isn't in the game at all.

Jack visited our home. We served coffee, and offered him a biscuit from a tin which contained many varieties. He picked one, took a bite from it, then laid it down on the table. He took another, sampled it like the first and put it down too. The third he liked, and he ate that. He must have reckoned he had the right to try all of them but eat only the biscuits which were particularly to his taste. We were taken aback by Jack's bad manners. Some think they can pick out the parts of Christianity they like and leave the rest. Mission is tough. It costs. It takes effort; it can be awkward and embarrassing; it means long-term involvement with people we wouldn't choose as friends. Some don't like that, so they keep the parts of Christianity they want and put mission aside.

Jesus didn't allow that. He didn't reckon these people were his Father's children, and he didn't know them.

> Not everyone who says to me, 'Lord, Lord,' will enter the kingdom of heaven, but only he who does the will of my Father who is in heaven. Many will say to me on that day, 'Lord, Lord, did we not prophesy in your name, and in your name drive out demons and perform many miracles?' Then I will tell them plainly, 'I never knew you. Away from me, you evildoers!' (Matt. 7:21–3)

Scary words, but words of Jesus. It seems there are some who are not badly born into God's family, they're not born into it at all.

Making the abnormal normal

For those who are in God's family mission is a natural instinct. It's not false, forced or even reluctant. It's the outworking of God's new nature in them. God loves lost people; God's children love lost people too.

Just because it's natural doesn't make it easy. There are lots of pressures, lots of obstacles, lots of dangers. (Breathing is always natural but it's hard to do in a smoke-filled room.) Yet mission is what God's life in the Christian craves to do. It's normality.

For too long we've accepted not loving and not serving as normal, and thus allowed the abnormal to be normal. The real normality needs to be restored, and for God's child that will mean a belief in mission, a passion for mission, and a life of mission. It'll be utterly natural, for it'll be the Father's own love flowing through his children.

Chapter 2

Mission isn't optional

TWO IDEAS HAVE virtually gained the status of gods for today's generation. One is tolerance. There is virtually nothing – no belief, no action, no lifestyle – which shouldn't be accepted. The other is freedom. We must be free to think and do whatever we please, to opt in or opt out as it suits us.

The second of these makes concepts like duty, loyalty and necessity seem old-fashioned. Out the window go sacrifice, commitment and obligation. So people opt out of marriage because 'it doesn't feel good' any more. It may have lasted fifteen years. There may be two or three children. But there must be freedom to change. It's unreasonable to tie anyone down, especially if it involves a long-term cost. Likewise just about every book and record club in the country has a falling level of membership. Most people don't want to be locked into having to buy each month or from each issue of the catalogue, not even for a limited time. Some clubs have had to drop any ongoing commitment and hope their initial and later bargains are enough to keep customers ordering. Obligation is out. Freedom is in.

We don't escape that modern mindset when it comes to mission. We'll witness if we want to witness, when we want to witness, to whom we want to witness, and we won't if it doesn't feel good or right for us. What's decisive is my gain or loss. The scales must dip on my side.

The scales rarely do when it comes to mission. Since witness always costs, few ever feel good about it or gain from it. Only masochists relish the sacrifice, unpopularity, criticism and other negatives that go with speaking up for Christ. So, since we've got the freedom to witness or not witness, often it doesn't get done.

The Great Commission

Therefore go and make disciples of all nations, baptising them in the name of the Father and of the Son and of the Holy Spirit, and teaching them to obey everything I have commanded you. And surely I am with you always, to the very end of the age.   Matt. 28:19–20

The Great Commission has become the Great Omission. Jesus spoke of making disciples of all nations; we do little to make disciples of any nation. He talked of complete commitment; we negotiate terms. He required lives to be trained for service; we make that an optional and unusual extra. He promised his presence; we live as if we were on our own.

Announce an evangelistic service or visitation programme and it scores a five-star groan factor from a congregation. Few actually speak against evangelism, of course, for how can anyone argue against reaching out to the lost? But there's more than one way to vote. The vast majority show what they feel by being distinctly absent when the event comes round. If asked, the explanations are forthcoming: 'I'm so busy something had to go'; 'I didn't have any non-Christian friends I could invite'; 'It's not my gift'; 'I stayed home and prayed for you'; 'I don't like that style of event.' Some of these reasons probably have legitimacy. But when they're quoted every time, and only the same faithful few turn up, it seems the many have opted out of mission. They're glad the few are doing it and feel bad they're not, but they'll swallow down their guilt by serving Jesus in other ways.

It's not that easy. Unfashionable it may be, but there are things which are not optional. Mission is one of them.

There are four senses in which mission has to be done.

I. It's commanded

You're driving faster than the speed limit and not only God but the police have noticed. They pull you over, check your licence, and tell you, 'You were doing 70 and the speed limit here is only 30.'

'Yes, but that's all right, officer,' you reply confidently, 'for I don't observe speed limits.'

'I'm so sorry. I hadn't realised that the law didn't apply to you,' the policeman replies, putting away his notebook and waving you on.

Does he? Does the law not apply to you if you don't care for it? I think not. The rules of the road aren't voluntary. They're not just for fanatics who like to add spice to their driving experience. Nor are they principles we can opt into or out of when it suits. They're laws. Compliance is required of us.

The New Testament is not a book of laws, but neither is it a book of suggestions and encouragements. It has commands, commands which we do not have the right to set aside.

Plenty of these commands are about mission.

- 'Therefore go and make disciples of all nations' (Matt. 28:19).
- 'He said to them, "Go into all the world and preach the good news to all creation" ' (Mark 16:15).
- 'Repentance and forgiveness of sins will be preached in his name to all nations, beginning at Jerusalem. You are witnesses of these things' (Luke 24:47–8).
- 'You did not choose me, but I chose you and appointed you to go and bear fruit – fruit that will last' (John 15:16).
- 'But you will receive power when the Holy Spirit comes on you; and you will be my witnesses in Jerusalem, and in all Judea and Samaria, and to the ends of the earth' (Acts 1:8).

The early disciples never considered they had any option about evangelising. At times they were faced with what must have seemed a choice between life and death according to whether they kept quiet or spoke up. There could be only one answer for them. 'Peter and John replied, "Judge for yourselves whether it is right in God's sight to obey you rather than God. For we cannot help speaking about what we have seen and heard" ' (Acts 4:19–20). They had to obey God. The gospel had to be told. People needed to know who Jesus was and what he had done. Silence was not possible.

Commands are not options. Jesus did not invite people to define their own discipleship, shape their lifestyles to suit personal wishes and compile their own agenda of things to do for God. They were to do what *he* said. They were to follow *his* agenda. 'If you love me, you will obey what I command' (John 14:15). Among his commands was certainly mission. We are ordered to make Jesus known.

2. It's the truth

Here's another other reason the apostles could not simply keep quiet when threatened. Common sense said they should. They'd seen Jesus crucified. They knew the authorities wouldn't hesitate to get rid of them too. Faced with what they faced, I'd have been thinking up a good reason why God needed me out of jail to serve him somewhere else. I'm sure I could have found spiritual backing for my self-preservation instinct. Not the apostles. After Peter' and John's first run in with the Sanhedrin, they kept on preaching and healing the sick. Great crowds flocked into Jerusalem to be on the receiving end of the apostles' ministry. More trouble was sure to come. They'd blatantly defied the Sanhedrin's orders, and they were successfully persuading people to believe in a man those Jewish leaders had crucified. It was too much. All the apostles were arrested and thrown in jail this time. They must have thought they'd soon be hanging on crosses. During the night an angel released them. It could have been their chance to escape. The angel had other ideas: ' "Go, stand in the temple courts," he said, "and tell the people the full message of this new life" ' (Acts 5:20).

They did. When the Sanhedrin gathered and ordered the apostles to be fetched from jail, of course they weren't there. They were preaching in one of the most public and strategic places in the city. This did not rejoice the Sanhedrin's hearts! The apostles were rearrested and brought before them. Their danger is clear in the high priest's words. ' "We gave you strict orders not to teach in this name," he said. "Yet you have filled Jerusalem with your teaching and are determined to make us guilty of this man's blood" ' (Acts 5:28).

The answer from the disciples was uncompromising:

Peter and the other apostles replied: 'We must obey God rather than men! The God of our fathers raised Jesus from the dead – whom you had killed by hanging him on a tree. God exalted him to his own right hand as Prince and Saviour that he might give repentance and forgiveness of sins to Israel. We are witnesses of these things, and so is the Holy Spirit, whom God has given to those who obey him' (Acts 5:29–32).

Those words were as good as signatures on their own execution orders. The Sanhedrin was furious and wanted to put the apostles to death, and it was only the intervention of Gamaliel that saved them. The apostles got off with a flogging and another warning. They left rejoicing they had been able to suffer for Jesus's sake – and kept right on witnessing: 'Day after day, in the temple courts and from house to house, they never stopped teaching and proclaiming the good news that Jesus is the Christ' (Acts 5:42).

They had to. They did it not only because they were under God's orders but because this was the truth. God had raised Jesus from the dead; he was Prince and Saviour; he was the way to forgiveness of sins. They knew it. They were witnesses. They had to tell.

If they hadn't been sure about Jesus, or if what he'd said and done had been insignificant, perhaps they could have chosen to keep quiet. Their wellbeing would have been more important than taking the risk of preaching. But what they knew about Jesus was world-changing. It was of eternal significance for every man, woman and child. They believed it with all their hearts. It was reality.

Ultimately everyone must live with reality. After something like a bereavement we're patient for a long time with people who can't come to terms with reality. A widow still sets a place at table for her husband; a parent won't touch the toys and clothes of the child who has died. When people are going through inner agony, we allow them time to adjust to the new situation. But eventually they must, and we get help for them if they can't face reality. Everyone must live with the truth.

That's what the apostles were doing. No matter how many threats, no matter how severe the threats, nothing changed the reality that Jesus was God's Saviour, was alive after death, and this gospel needed to be believed by all people. That was the truth.

It's still the truth, and it's a truth that makes mission compulsive. If we really believe it we must tell it. It can be inconvenient and dangerous, but it's reality and we must live in reality.

3. There's a moral obligation

If someone was terminally ill but found a cure, surely he'd tell others who had the same illness. That's one of the oldest and most common illustrations preachers use about evangelism. The basis of it is the moral imperative of telling something you know that others need to know.

A classic biblical example is in 2 Kings 7. Samaria is besieged by the Arameans, and the Israelites are on the point of being starved to death or into surrender. Four lepers decide to make the best of two bad choices. If they stay in the embattled city they'll die with everyone else. If they leave and surrender to the Arameans, they'll probably die but there's just a chance they'll be shown mercy. So, at nightfall, they go to the Aramean camp. To their astonishment they find it deserted. Earlier that day God had caused the Arameans to hear the sounds of an attacking army, and they'd fled, leaving everything behind them. The lepers are saved! They begin to eat, drink and stash away the Arameans' treasure.

But not for long. 'Then they said to each other, "We're not doing right. This is a day of good news and we are keeping it to ourselves. If we wait until daylight, punishment will overtake us. Let's go at once and report this to the royal palace" ' (2 Kings 7:9).

Perhaps the lepers' motivation should have been concern for others, rather than fear of being punished, but, either way, they knew they *ought* to pass on the news. They would be wrong to keep it to themselves.

Likewise to know the truth about Jesus, to believe him to be the only way to the Father, and *not* to tell others about him is culpable selfishness.

A man is walking by a river, sees a child fall into the water, hears his cries for help but, though he can swim, walks on and leaves the child to drown. How would public opinion react to that? Would people not think the man callous? Would they not virtually blame him for the child's death since he could have saved him but didn't? They probably would.

We don't usually think in such extreme terms with people being lost because of our failure to tell the gospel. But is it different? We know, they don't. We keep quiet, they never get the chance of salvation. It jars and disturbs when written like that. And there are complex theological issues involved. But there's no escaping a moral obligation to pass on the cure we've found to mankind's terminal illness.

4. There's a heritage to be shared

There's a family of words used in the Bible to describe the gospel as some form of heritage which has become ours. Matthew 13:44 says, 'The kingdom of heaven is like treasure,' and 1 Corinthians 4:2 says Christians are 'those who have been given a trust'. Terms like deposit, possession, inheritance are also there.

How do people react to being made responsible for something of immense importance? If my father left me a legacy of a fifty-bedroom mansion of the finest architecture, lavishly decorated with works of art and furnished with invaluable antique bookcases, carpets and chairs, I'd try to maintain it. If I looked after it well, rather than letting it fall into ruin, I'd feel I was discharging my responsibility for the family heritage.

That's not the New Testament idea. The gospel heritage is for reproduction, not preservation.

The *locus classicus* for that is the parable of the talents. The talents (units of coinage) weren't owned by the servants; the money belonged to the master. Although we're not told the conversation between master and servants when the money was handed over, clearly he expected them to use it. Two took risks, risks which paid off, and they doubled the amount they'd been given. One didn't. He neither lost the money nor abused it. He simply preserved it. Whether he was frightened (as he claimed) or just lazy, his only plan was to make sure the money was still there when his master came back. The day came, and the servants were sent for. The risk-taking and gain of the first two were commended and rewarded. The preservation mentality of the other servant was condemned and he was dismissed.

That parable appears in a section of Jesus's teaching about the kingdom of heaven and what it takes to be qualified for admission. Is Jesus saying those who don't spread the gospel won't get into heaven? He could be. But that would be a very hard line for him to take and a narrow interpretation for us to make. There's more to reproducing the Christian life than telling others about Jesus. He's

The Parable of the Talents

Again, it will be like a man going on a journey, who called his servants and entrusted his property to them. To one he gave five talents of money, to another two talents, and to another one talent, each according to his ability. Then he went on his journey. The man who had received the five talents went at once and put his money to work and gained five more. So also, the one with the two talents gained two more. But the man who had received the one talent went off, dug a hole in the ground and hid his master's money.

After a long time the master of those servants returned and settled accounts with them. The man who had received the five talents brought the other five. 'Master,' he said, 'you entrusted me with five talents. See, I have gained five more.'

His master replied, 'Well done, good and faithful servant! You have been faithful with a few things; I will put you in charge of many things. Come and share your master's happiness!'

The man with the two talents also came. 'Master,' he said, 'you entrusted me with two talents; see, I have gained two more.'

His master replied, 'Well done, good and faithful servant! You have been faithful with a few things; I will put you in charge of many things. Come and share your master's happiness!'

Then the man who had received the one talent came. 'Master,' he said, 'I knew that you are a hard man, harvesting where you have not sown and gathering where you have not scattered seed. So I was afraid and went out and hid your talent in the ground. See, here is what belongs to you.'

His master replied, 'You wicked, lazy servant! So you knew that I harvest where I have not sown and gather where I have not scattered seed? Well then, you should have put my money on deposit with the bankers, so that

> when I returned I would have received it back with interest.
> 'Take the talent from him and give it to the one who has
> the ten talents. For everyone who has will be given more,
> and he will have an abundance. Whoever does not have,
> even what he has will be taken from him. And throw that
> worthless servant outside, into the darkness, where there
> will be weeping and gnashing of teeth.'
>
> Matt. 25:14–30

probably talking about our response to the whole of the investment God has put into us. But that investment includes the gospel message, and our efforts or lack of them to share that message will be judged. These are strong words. It's clearly unacceptable to do nothing with the treasure God has given us. Merely keeping the gospel as a private possession won't do. It's for us, but not only us.

William Carey saw that in the late eighteenth century. As a cobbler turned pastor, he wanted others to know the gospel which had saved him, including those in 'heathen' lands. Among the Calvinistic Particular Baptists, to which Carey belonged, he wasn't the only one to value the gospel, nor the only one to believe people of all nations could be saved. But the more nearly unique thing about Carey was his belief that it was the responsibility of Christians 'here' to tell those 'there'. When he agitated at meetings for the formation of a missionary society, others at first couldn't see the need. Supposedly he was told, 'Sit down, young man! When God chooses to convert the heathen he will do it without your aid or mine.' That was probably never said, but it fairly reflects the view of many at that time. But Carey had grasped that God's way of bringing salvation was through the actions of those already Christians. Hence he penned his 'Enquiry into the Obligations of Christians to use means for the Conversion of the Heathens'. The key word in the title is 'means', that Christians actually had to do something to communicate the gospel. Eventually a number were persuaded, and thus what is known today as the Baptist Missionary Society was formed in 1792.

One of my favourite children's talks is to show a box of chocolates, tell the kids that these have been donated for everyone to enjoy, but then stand there eating each one myself. That generates great angst, even among those who don't like chocolates. There's indignation that something meant for everyone is being eaten by just one person. The gospel is God's gift to everyone. Its benefits are not only for me. I've got to share it.

I believe in mission, and believe that mission isn't optional. It's not optional whether people need to know of Jesus, and it's not optional whether I need to tell them. God commands me to witness, and even if he hadn't, love for the lost would demand it.

I once saw a child nearly drown. He'd fallen into a river, and couldn't scramble out. That lad screamed for help as if he was using up his last breath. He probably thought he was. I wasn't first to help. Like a sprinter from his blocks came the boy's father. He ran to the river bank, grabbed his son's outstretched hand, pulled him clear and then held him fast. Love reacted to need. It could never have done anything else. The boy was in great danger. Fast as he could his father came to save him.

The obligation for mission is no different to that.

Chapter 3

Not for the faint-hearted

I WASN'T EXPECTING a near-death experience. All the minister had asked us to do was friendship evangelism. We were to knock on doors in our area, offer the love of our church and take any opportunity to share the gospel.

So Peggy and I had spent a more or less profitable evening round the tenement flats nearby. Some had talked to us, many hadn't. No-one had invited us in.

Until this one. A craggy old face peered round the door in response to our knocking. 'Yesss . . . ?' came a squeaky, high-pitched voice.

We explained that we were Christians offering friendship to our community. 'Come in then,' the elderly woman said immediately. Peggy gave me an encouraging smile. At last.

The home was far from affluent. Far from clean, actually, but perhaps this lonely old soul specially needed our friendship. 'I'll show you photos of my family,' she said to Peggy. I got my instructions too. 'You can mend my telly.'

It seemed irrelevant to point out that I knew nothing about electronics. Perhaps it just needed tuning. I looked at her ancient television set, which was hardly the cutting edge of technology. As though I knew what I was doing, I began twiddling the large dials on the set. Meanwhile Peggy sat by the open fire nodding appreciatively while the woman went through the contents of several photo albums and explained who was who. 'Great Aunt Maggie married her second cousin Bert. He was too young for her, but they had five children . . .' I admired Peggy's patience as a succession of family connections and one or two scandals were described in detail.

Bang! An immense blast deafened me, and a mighty rushing wind nearly swept me off my feet. Doors slammed, the window rattled, the walls shook, dust rose in the air. This was not a blessing of the Holy Spirit, but it was nearly a rapid launch to meet Jesus. As the dust settled and we regathered our wits we realised we'd been in the middle of an explosion. It transpired our elderly hostess had been lighting her gas cooker when we'd rung the doorbell. She'd left the gas turned on but unlit when she'd answered. Gradually, while Peggy had looked at photos and I'd tried to fix the TV, gas had built up in her kitchenette, seeped into the main room and been ignited eventually by the open fire. The old lady didn't seem too perturbed. We were very perturbed. Our evangelism had been nearly terminal. And she didn't even come to church.

We might have paid a high price for mission. The idea that evangelism may hurt is an unpopular and, usually, unacceptable notion today. We want cost-free, risk-free witness. We'd like to share our faith, but with no loss of popularity, career, comfort or pleasure. We'll search for the method that works painlessly. We'll wait until witness can be done easily. Any sacrifice had better be no more than having to wait until you get home from the mission event to watch the video-taped version of the football match.

> At the last moment before sailing, I was asked if I would pledge myself to remain ten years unmarried. This question took me by surprise, as I had not thought much of that subject, but had merely considered it would be risky to take a wife into the interior, then as little known as the wilds of Africa. I replied that whether I would marry in ten days or ten years would depend on what was best for the work. It fell out that I did not marry for nine years.
>
> Timothy Richard, China missionary
> *Forty-five Years in China: Reminiscences*
> (T. Fisher Unwin, 1916)

The 'Will you agree not to marry for ten years?' question put to Timothy Richard by his mission agency as he was leaving for service in China in 1869 is remarkable to modern minds for two reasons. The first is that it was ever asked. Today it would be considered impertinent and intrusive for a mission agency to suggest whether or not someone should marry. The second is Richard's reply. He didn't tell the agency to 'Mind your own business.' Nor did he say something to the effect, 'I will marry whenever I fall in love.' He said that when he would marry would depend on what was best for the missionary work. If having a wife better enabled him to do mission, he'd marry. If being single was better, he'd stay as he was. For Richard, the missionary task had priority and his marital state had to fit. He was putting mission needs above personal wants. Many would reverse those today.

Must mission be done even when it costs? What's reasonable? If witnessing would damage a friendship or diminish a reputation, is that the price that has to be paid? If mission means a life is at risk, is that an acceptable sacrifice? These are not theoretical questions. Every day Christians decide whether or not to open their mouths to neighbours, colleagues and friends, knowing that their words may not be liked. Should they witness no matter how unpopular? Missionaries go into dangerous countries because often that's where the gospel most needs to be heard and experienced. Should they be there if it means they could be hurt or die?

There is, thankfully, no lack of biblical teaching from which to deduce at least some answers.

The Old Testament

From the earliest pages of the Bible's story, God's servants faced risk doing his work. Abraham's journeyings took him to unsafe places. At one time he thought his life would be threatened because he had a good-looking wife. 'As he was about to enter Egypt, he said to his wife Sarai, "I know what a beautiful woman you are. When the Egyptians see you, they will say, 'This is his wife.' Then they will kill me but will let you live. Say you are my sister, so that I will be treated well for your sake and my life will be spared because of you" ' (Gen. 12:11–13).

Joseph nearly died for dreaming the future God had for him or, rather, telling those dreams to his brothers. ' "Here comes that dreamer!" they said to each other. "Come now, let's kill him and throw him into one of these cisterns and say that a ferocious animal devoured him. Then we'll see what comes of his dreams" ' (Gen. 37:19–20).

Men like Samson did lose their lives fighting for God. 'Samson said, "Let me die with the Philistines!" Then he pushed with all his might, and down came the temple on the rulers and all the people in it. Thus he killed many more when he died than while he lived' (Judg. 16:30).

As Israel faced battles against neighbouring enemies, there was a constant need for God's people to put their lives on the line. A classic is David in his confrontation with Goliath.

He looked David over and saw that he was only a boy, ruddy and handsome, and he despised him. He said to David, 'Am I a dog, that you come at me with sticks?' And the Philistine cursed David by his gods. 'Come here,' he said, 'and I'll give your flesh to the birds of the air and the beasts of the field!'

David said to the Philistine, 'You come against me with sword and spear and javelin, but I come against you in the name of the LORD Almighty, the God of the armies of Israel, whom you have defied. This day the LORD will hand you over to me, and I'll strike you down and cut off your head. Today I will give the carcasses of the Philistine army to the birds of the air and the beasts of the earth, and the whole world will know that there is a God in Israel. All those gathered here will know that it is not by sword or spear that the LORD saves; for the battle is the LORD's, and he will give all of you into our hands.'

As the Philistine moved closer to attack him, David ran quickly towards the battle line to meet him. Reaching into his bag and taking out a stone, he slung it and struck the Philistine on the forehead. The stone sank into his forehead, and he fell face down on the ground.

So David triumphed over the Philistine with a sling and a stone; without a sword in his hand he struck down the Philistine and killed him. (1 Sam. 17:42–50)

In Israel's eyes, as David says, battles like these were not ordinary flesh–and–blood struggles between warring nations. The Philistines were enemies of God, and David's battle against Goliath was God's fight against the forces of evil which opposed him.

That's even clearer when the person standing alone before many enemies is Elijah. He set a test between him and Baal's prophets. Who the real God was over Israel would be proved according to which God lit a sacrifice miraculously. Baal's prophets pranced and chanted all day, but with no success. Then it was Elijah's turn. With drama and courage by the bucketful, he had the sacrifice drenched in water first. Then came the moment.

> At the time of sacrifice, the prophet Elijah stepped forward and prayed: 'O LORD, God of Abraham, Isaac and Israel, let it be known today that you are God in Israel and that I am your servant and have done all these things at your command. Answer me, O LORD, answer me, so these people will know that you, O LORD, are God, and that you are turning their hearts back again.'
>
> Then the fire of the LORD fell and burned up the sacrifice, the wood, the stones and the soil, and also licked up the water in the trench.
>
> When all the people saw this, they fell prostrate and cried, 'The LORD – he is God! The LORD – he is God!'
>
> Then Elijah commanded them, 'Seize the prophets of Baal. Don't let anyone get away!' They seized them, and Elijah had them brought down to the Kishon Valley and slaughtered there. (1 Kings 18:36–40)

Elijah's purpose was evangelistic. He wanted his people's hearts turned back to God, and entered this battle so that would happen. He put his life on the line for their salvation. The prophets of Baal died, but if God hadn't sent fire from heaven it would have been Elijah's life which would have ended in the Kishon Valley. That was the risk he took to turn his nation back to God.

So the stories go on. Sometimes, as for Jeremiah, the enemy is from within. 'The priests, the prophets and all the people heard Jeremiah speak these words in the house of the LORD. But as soon as Jeremiah finished telling all the people everything the LORD had commanded him to say, the priests, the prophets and all the people seized him and said, "You must die!" ' (Jer. 26:7–8). He didn't die, though there were times when he came close to it for persisting with prophecies which were unpopular.

These people at risk were not stepping out of God's will. They weren't in trouble because they went their own way, perhaps with a spiritual bravado which exceeded common sense. Rather, they got into danger precisely because God put them there. He sent them to speak and act for him and it cost them dearly.

The New Testament

Persecution of the first Christians was inevitable. If people were prepared to crucify Jesus, they'd certainly kill them too if they continued his work. Not only did they carry it on and grow in numbers and influence, they preached the offensive and near-blasphemous message that God's Messiah had been rejected and put to death by the very people who ought to have recognised and welcomed him: 'You handed him over to be killed, and you disowned him before Pilate, though he had decided to let him go. You disowned the Holy and Righteous One and asked that a murderer be released to you. You killed the author of life, but God raised him from the dead. We are witnesses of this' (Acts 3:13–15).

When Peter and John and then all the apostles were arrested, their line was uncompromising: 'We must obey God rather than men! We are witnesses of these things, and so is the Holy Spirit, whom God has given to those who obey him' (Acts 5:29, 32). What they knew to be right wasn't going to change just because it was inconvenient for their personal safety. They had no love greater than their love for God, no loyalty greater than their loyalty to him, no ambition greater than their ambition to serve him. Nothing was more important than speaking for Jesus. And if speaking for Jesus cost them their lives, so be it.

Before long a Christian did pay with his life because of his witness: Stephen. He was an effective evangelist. In a sense that was the problem.

Opposition arose, however, from members of the Synagogue of the Freedmen (as it was called) – Jews of Cyrene and Alexandria as well as the provinces of Cilicia and Asia. These men began to argue with Stephen, but they could not stand up against his wisdom or the Spirit by whom he spoke.

Then they secretly persuaded some men to say, 'We have

heard Stephen speak words of blasphemy against Moses and against God.'

So they stirred up the people and the elders and the teachers of the law. They seized Stephen and brought him before the Sanhedrin. (Acts 6:9–12)

At that moment Stephen had a choice. He could back down, apologise for having upset anyone, and promise not to cause a nuisance by continuing to speak so openly about Jesus of Nazareth. Probably that would have been enough for him to escape. He would have been allowed to go on believing whatever he liked privately.

Stephen couldn't do that. His faith was not private, and the truth about Jesus had to be told. So when the Sanhedrin put him on trial he preached his message to them. He finished his address by holding them responsible for killing God's Messiah, and said he could see Jesus standing at the right hand of God. That was the final straw. A form of mob madness broke out.

One of those responsible for Stephen's death became Christianity's early missionary to foreign parts. The kind of suffering he once inflicted he later experienced.

I have worked much harder, been in prison more frequently, been flogged more severely, and been exposed to death again and again. Five times I received from the Jews the forty lashes minus one. Three times I was beaten with rods, once I was stoned, three times I was shipwrecked, I spent a night and a day in the open sea, I have been constantly on the move. I have been in danger from rivers, in danger from bandits, in danger from my own countrymen, in danger from Gentiles; in danger in the city, in danger in the country, in danger at sea; and in danger from false brothers. I have laboured and toiled and have often gone without sleep; I have known hunger and thirst and have often gone without food; I have been cold and naked. Besides everything else, I face daily the pressure of my concern for all the churches.

2 Cor. 11:23–8

At this they covered their ears and, yelling at the top of their voices, they all rushed at him, dragged him out of the city and began to stone him. Meanwhile, the witnesses laid their clothes at the feet of a young man named Saul.

While they were stoning him, Stephen prayed, 'Lord Jesus, receive my spirit.' Then he fell on his knees and cried out, 'Lord, do not hold this sin against them.' When he had said this, he fell asleep. (Acts 7:57–60)

Stephen died an unjust and cruel death. All he'd done was tell people about Jesus. He'd given them the chance of eternal life. He'd shared the gospel for their good. But they didn't want to hear, and they killed him.

Stephen stands at the head of a long line of martyrs for Christianity. Most of the first apostles are thought to have died for their faith. James, brother of John, was executed by the sword on King Herod's instructions (Acts 12:2). Peter is reputed to have died in Rome. Paul probably died in one of Nero's persecutions of Christians in Rome. Ancient records say he was beheaded, but he could have been one of those Nero had tarred, hung on poles and then set on fire to light his garden.

The Great Fire of Rome took place in July 64. Nero, the Emperor, was widely suspected of having caused the fire, so he looked for a scapegoat. The Christians were a soft target.

Mockery of every sort was added to their deaths. Covered with the skins of beasts, they were torn by dogs and perished, or were nailed to crosses, or were doomed to the flames. These served to illuminate the night when daylight faded. Nero had thrown open his gardens for the spectacle, and was exhibiting a show in the circus, while he mingled with the people in the dress of a charioteer or drove about in a chariot. Hence, even for criminals who deserved extreme and exemplary punishment, there arose a feeling of compassion; for it was not, as it seemed, for the public good, but to glut one man's cruelty, that they were being destroyed.

Tacitus, *Annals*, XV.44.6–8

The danger for the early Christians was twofold. Their message was profoundly offensive to Jews, claiming this crucified man Jesus was really God's Messiah. They also rejected the divine right claimed by the Roman Emperor. They refused to kneel to him as a god, call him 'Lord' and offer sacrifice to him. For them there was only one Lord, Jesus. That made them disloyal citizens of the Empire, and many were put to death for their unyielding and inflexible allegiance to Jesus. The gruesome and painful forms of execution used were undoubtedly to satisfy sadistic lusts in the spectators, but also to deter others from holding such exclusive Christian beliefs.

Martyrdom is normal

Martyrdom stories make dramatic reading, and everyone loves heroes. But everyone doesn't love martyrdom. Therefore it's more than a little tempting to exclude ourselves from that possibility by deciding that martyrdom is only for very special Christians, the superheroes of the faith, the kind God calls to dangerous places or to come to the fore at dangerous times. I'm no superhero, not one of God's marines, so martyrdom has nothing to do with me.

But it has. Jesus defined martyrdom as part of normal Christianity: 'You will receive power when the Holy Spirit comes on you; and you will be my witnesses in Jerusalem, and in all Judea and Samaria, and to the ends of the earth' (Acts 1:8). Jesus told his followers they would be witnesses. 'Witness' is a translation of the Greek word *martus*, a word used in law courts for someone called to give evidence. It's also the word from which we get 'martyr'. Its meaning of 'someone who gives his or her life for a cause' arises in part because so often a witness suffered for speaking up, in this case for Christ.

That's explicitly how the word is used in Paul's testimony in Acts 22:20: 'And when the blood of your martyr Stephen was shed, I stood there giving my approval and guarding the clothes of those who were killing him.'

The writer of Revelation uses *martus* or *marturia* (often translated 'testimony') with the same connotation.

I know where you live – where Satan has his throne. Yet you

remain true to my name. You did not renounce your faith in me, even in the days of Antipas, my faithful witness, who was put to death in your city – where Satan lives. (Rev. 2:13)

When he opened the fifth seal, I saw under the altar the souls of those who had been slain because of the word of God and the testimony they had maintained. (Rev. 6:9)

I saw that the woman was drunk with the blood of the saints, the blood of those who bore testimony to Jesus. (Rev. 17:6)

I saw thrones on which were seated those who had been given authority to judge. And I saw the souls of those who had been beheaded because of their testimony for Jesus and because of the word of God. They had not worshipped the beast or his image and had not received his mark on their foreheads or their hands. They came to life and reigned with Christ for a thousand years. (Rev. 20:4)

The same family of words with the same emphasis keeps recurring. By no means did every Christian in New Testament times suffer or die for having faith in Jesus. But to be a witness was to be a martyr, and any Christian had to be willing to accept the price of discipleship. As Jesus had been persecuted so might anyone following him.

Always in the plan
Suffering was not a surprise for the early Christians. Jesus had always said that following him would be costly. 'He said to them all: "If anyone would come after me, he must deny himself and take up his cross daily and follow me" ' (Luke 9:23). We're remote from the first century of the Roman Empire, but to those who lived in it those words of Jesus were strong and probably frightening. He was inviting them to accept a death sentence. People who took up the cross went on a one-way journey to death. No-one ever returned. All right, this is imagery, but it's powerful imagery of hardship and suffering.

Words like those from Jesus were not unique. He made sure people knew discipleship would be no sinecure. He wasn't offering feather beds on which believers could recline and await translation to glory. Over and over he stressed they would have a hard time as his followers. There would be difficulties, suffering and opposition.

> Blessed are those who are persecuted because of righteousness, for theirs is the kingdom of heaven.
> Blessed are you when people insult you, persecute you and falsely say all kinds of evil against you because of me. (Matt. 5:10–11)

> Pray for those who persecute you. (Matt. 5:44)

> Go! I am sending you out like lambs among wolves. (Luke 10:3)

> I tell you, my friends, do not be afraid of those who kill the body and after that can do no more. (Luke 12:4)

> Do you think I came to bring peace on earth? No, I tell you, but division. From now on there will be five in one family divided against each other, three against two and two against three. They will be divided, father against son and son against father, mother against daughter and daughter against mother, mother-in-law against daughter-in-law and daughter-in-law against mother-in-law. (Luke 12:51–3)

> But before all this, they will lay hands on you and persecute you. They will deliver you to synagogues and prisons, and you will be brought before kings and governors, and all on account of my name. This will result in your being witnesses to them. You will be betrayed even by parents, brothers, relatives and friends, and they will put some of you to death. All men will hate you because of me. But not a hair of your head will perish. By standing firm you will gain life. (Luke 21:12–13, 16–19)

> If the world hates you, keep in mind that it hated me first. If you belonged to the world, it would love you as its own. As it is, you do not belong to the world, but I have chosen you out of the world. That is why the world hates you. Remember the words I spoke to you: 'No servant is greater than his master.' If they persecuted me, they will persecute you also. If they obeyed my

teaching, they will obey yours also. They will treat you this way because of my name, for they do not know the One who sent me. (John 15:18–21)

A time is coming, and has come, when you will be scattered, each to his own home . . . I have told you these things, so that in me you may have peace. In this world you will have trouble. (John 16:32–3)

Reading these words, you wouldn't think Jesus was conducting a recruiting campaign! He certainly gave no sales pitch with only the up-side of discipleship mentioned. He knew that those who identified with him would face as many difficulties and as much opposition as he had. No-one should come into discipleship under false pretences.

Discipleship's bottom line

> When Christ calls a man he bids him come and die.
> Dietrich Bonhoeffer
> *The Cost of Discipleship*

The bottom line of discipleship, then, is willingness to pay any price and suffer any cost. Personal agendas get set aside. Self-interest goes on the back burner. Discipleship is about accepting God's rule, entering God's service, living on God's terms, engaging in God's mission. Far from being risk-free and cost-free, Christianity requires disciples to walk by faith and give up all the values and priorities of this world including life itself.

Hence Christians have died rather than deny their Saviour. For some that's been the choice of a particular moment when persecuted. Others have made deliberate, long-term choices that put them at risk.

It's impossible, for example, to read the statistics of illness and death among those who set sail last century for the Congo, and not be moved. I'm stirred by the courage and sacrifice of those who went first. I'm almost more moved that when news seeped home of their deaths, others went to take their place.

> Yours of November 22 to hand two days since. Also the sad news of the death of our brother Davies. We are very, very downhearted about all these losses at Wathen. I am indeed sorry for his parents. The loss after loss the Wathen staff have had of late must make them feel very, very lonely. Dr Webb and Philip Davies dead; Cameron at the gates of death, and Bentley very sick, within one short year, is a series that brings a train of most serious thoughts.
>
> Letter of George Grenfell from Bolobo, Congo,
> 23 December 1895

The dangers were huge. When Stanley entered Africa in 1874 he was with three other white men and had over 350 porters. Within three years he was the only white man left and the porters numbered only 114. Fever, dysentery, battles, kidnapping, floods and starvation had wiped out more than two-thirds of their number. Into those same conditions were going missionaries tough in spirit but desperately unprotected in body. In 1876 my own Baptist Missionary Society sent twenty-four-year-old Thomas Comber to the Cameroons. Along with George Grenfell, he made some remarkably brave journeys into the heart of the Congo, sometimes attacked by cannibalistic tribes. After a couple of years he came back to Britain to report on progress and challenge more to come to that part of Africa. There were many chances to spread the gospel, but others were needed to share the work. In 1879 he returned, taking his young bride. They were in love, and looked forward to years of happiness. Neither saw them. His wife died within four months of arrival in Africa. In fact, within the first 40 years of BMS work in the Congo, 61 missionaries died. When Comber returned again to Britain in 1885 his frail body shocked audiences. He seemed like an old man, but was in fact only thirty-two. Yet his words reflected the spirit of those missionaries as he preached from the text 'Except a corn of wheat fall into the ground and die, it abideth alone: but if it die, it bringeth forth much fruit.' He sailed again to Africa but was dead within two years.

Our Society's history has other heart-rending stories. George Pople went as a missionary to Africa in 1893 but came home in

1895 and married Kate Matthews the following March. Two months later, in great health, they set off together for the Congo. During the following months he was thrown into hard work establishing a new base station. The effort seems to have lowered his resistance. Fever gripped him. For days he struggled for life, nursed by his heavily pregnant wife, but he died on 12 April 1897. Three weeks later Kate gave birth to a son but caught fever at the same time and died on 29 May. George was twenty-eight and Kate twenty-five. There was no-one in the Congo to care for the orphaned baby. Urgent plans were made to get him quickly back to Britain where his grandparents would look after him. He was given to William White and his wife, missionaries on their way home. But William was suffering from malaria. They reached the coast safely, got on the mail steamer *Niger* and set sail. But after only a short time the child took ill and died on 3 July. On 4 July William White died too, aged thirty-one. He and the baby were buried together in one coffin at Mayumba. The Baptist Handbook of 1898 finishes its report on the events with these words: 'So closed one of the most sorrowful pages in the record of our Congo Mission, and yet through such experiences the Kingdom of Christ sweeps on to its world-wide dominion.'

Without question these missionaries had immense courage. They knew before they went that there was a high likelihood they would die. Some are reputed to have packed their belongings in crates that could double as their coffins. They went because God had called them and the possibility or even probability of death was no reason not to obey.

There are other countries with stories as challenging. Not just missionaries but often every Christian in an area suffered. The beginning of the twentieth century saw the violent Boxer uprising in North China, particularly in Shansi province. Fanatical nationalists, stirred by the Empress-Dowager, attacked foreigners and local Christians associated with foreigners. Some 32,000 Chinese Christians died, plus about 185 missionaries and 53 missionary children. The cruelty was terrible. Mr Chao was a well-known Christian and friends told him to escape. But he wouldn't. He and his mother, sister and wife were taken to the local Boxer chief who ordered their deaths. Mr Chao was beheaded first with a huge knife used

Amongst many who sought to deter me [from being a missionary] was one dear old Christian gentleman, whose crowning argument always was, –

'The Cannibals! You will be eaten by Cannibals!'

At last I replied, 'Mr Dickson, you are advanced in years now and your own prospect is soon to be laid in the grave, there to be eaten by worms; I confess to you, that if I can but live and die serving and honouring the Lord Jesus, it will make no difference to me whether I am eaten by Cannibals or by worms; and in the Great Day my resurrection body will arise as fair as yours in the likeness of our risen Redeemer.'

The old gentleman, raising his hands in a deprecating attitude, left the room exclaiming, –

'After that I have nothing more to say!'

John G. Paton
Missionary to the New Hebrides: An Autobiography
(Hodder and Stoughton, 1889)

for chopping straw. The women were given the chance to recant and live, but they refused. The old mother said, 'You have killed my son; you can now kill me.' She was beheaded. The other women still refused to abandon their faith and one after the other they too died. In another place the Christians were worshipping when a mob burst in and set the building on fire. The evangelist in charge was hauled outside and beaten until he was unconscious. He partially recovered, was seen to be praying, and someone cried, 'See, he is praying even now! Drag him to the fire!' They held him, but before they could throw him in the flames he freed himself, and said, 'You do not need to drag me. I will go myself.' He walked into the burning building, the roof collapsed on him, and he died.

This is the price of mission. For most of us it's discipleship like we have either never known or forgotten. We think ourselves hard done by if someone frowns or laughs when we admit to being a Christian. Our hardships are rarely worse, but often merely knowing the mention of Jesus isn't popular is enough to keep us from opening our mouths. There are moments I feel ashamed of myself.

And others, too, had trial of cruel mocking. They were stoned to death, cut to pieces inch by inch, dismembered and disembowelled, saturated with oil and set on fire, hurled from precipices, drowned in rivers, buried alive in pits, decapitated, and broken on cart wheels – refusing to accept release with a nod or a word, because they believed in the resurrection. Endowed with power from on high, they were able to 'out-think, out-live and out-die the pagan'. Like Tertullian of old they could say, 'Go on; rack, torture, grind us into powder; our numbers increase as you mow us down. The blood of the Christians is seed.' These are they of whom the world is not worthy. They belong to the noble company of martyrs who have triumphed gloriously. By their faithfulness even unto death they not only received the crown of Life; they saved the Church in its hour of peril, and bequeathed to future generations a rich heritage of apostolic witness.

George A. Young, describing martyrdom during the Boxer Rebellion in China,
The Living Christ in Modern China
(Carey Kingsgate Press, 1947)

Mission taken seriously is important, but it isn't romantic. It costs, maybe everything. Strictly speaking, persecution and hardship are not the cost of mission; they're the cost of discipleship. They're part of what it is to have signed away your rights. When the battle's raging, and the commander's whistle blows for the troops to leave the trench and run towards the enemy, it's too late then for any soldier to debate whether or not he'll go, whether or not he's prepared to face a hail of bullets. His willingness to fight and even to die isn't open for renegotiation. It was settled the day he joined the army. Likewise for the Christian. 'You are not your own; you were bought at a price' (1 Cor. 6:19–20).

Much of modern life is self-orientated. We expect to gain something for ourselves – at least to feel good – from everything we do. If Christians are controlled by that instinct not much mission will get done. But Christians aren't self-orientated. We're Christorientated. We follow Jesus, whether or not we gain, whether or not we feel good about what we do. Following him involves us in a costly mission. It's costly for us because it was for him; the cost was his life. We can't have full discipleship at a discount price.

Paying the price

Of course, the price of mission gets paid usually in small amounts rather than one great sum. There's a cost here and a cost there. It costs on the biggest scale and the smallest scale, and there are many with the scars to prove it. Here's a miscellany of examples (by no means a complete list) of how the price of mission gets paid. Obviously the hardship varies according to where we live and what we do. But there are many ways in which comfort and self-interest are threatened or sacrificed. Life serving Jesus is tough.

Weariness

Many times I've been on or led special missions. Often I've talked with teenagers until the early hours of the morning, finally flopped on a rough mattress laid on the floor of a church hall, then got up at dawn for another day of evangelism. Frequently sleep has been disturbed. In the middle of one night a fellow broke in through my window. He wasn't trying to assault me or steal from the church, but he had amorous intentions towards one of the local girls he thought was staying with our mission team and had picked the window to the wrong room. Mission teams always have minimum sleep but expend maximum effort, a formula guaranteed to produce total exhaustion. Thankfully it's survivable in the short term.

For some exhaustion is a more permanent way of life. I've been in an isolated African town with missionaries who were known locally as people who'd help with problems. Late into the evening neighbours would come to their gate asking for things. Often all they wanted was aspirin. Any secular business would have ignored 'out of hours' callers, but my friends knew these people and cared for them. One of those shouts at the gate could have been because a mother had gone into a difficult labour, or a child was dying. They couldn't ignore these folk. But the missionaries lived permanently worn out, their tiredness often worsened in the hot season by the inability to sleep even when they were in bed. Paul's words,

'I have laboured and toiled and have often gone without sleep' (2 Cor. 11:27), made sense to them. Mission means weariness.

Threats
Stuart was the missionary for a church in a tough city area. He and his wife Maureen, plus their two-year-old daughter, lived in a run-down street with neighbours who weren't pillars of the local church. 'Exactly the people I want to reach,' he said. He was brave to be there. Almost everyone else would have moved out if they could.

Mostly Stuart made friends but the day came when he made an enemy. Something he said or did upset one of the local families. A whisper in Stuart's ear told him a bunch of lads would be round that night to burn him out. Maureen and their daughter were sent in haste out of the area because these people were to be taken seriously. Late that night Stuart sat at his kitchen table, half the time drinking coffee and half the time praying. By 3 a.m. he couldn't help closing his eyes. It was the brick through the window that jolted him awake. Before he'd a chance to phone for emergency help he heard the shout. In unrepeatable language, he was told to keep himself out of other people's business or next time it'd be a petrol bomb. He knew they meant it. In the weeks ahead Stuart tried to put the threat out of his mind. But he couldn't. Through the dark hours of the night he'd lie beside Maureen worrying about her, their daughter, and himself. He prayed for the fears to go away, but they didn't. Four months later he moved his family to a safer area many miles from the threats of that place.

Was Stuart a failure? Should he have trusted God more? Should he have been more willing to accept hostility and even injury in order to keep doing his missionary work? I have plenty of theoretical answers to questions like these. But if I'd been there with a wife and little girl, I wonder if I'd have done anything different from Stuart.

Threats come in many forms to those who witness, from potential loss of a friendship to violence or death. There are no easy responses. Whether it's fight or flight, for the threatened Christian there's hardship.

Career

For years Drew and Sharon knew God was calling them to overseas mission. For Sharon it virtually ran in the family. Her parents had been missionaries, her childhood filled with the importance of sharing the gospel with all the people of the world. Drew hadn't become a Christian until medical school. But soon after that he'd sensed God wanted him to use his skills for those who needed them most in the developing world.

Those skills were considerable. Drew had specialised in paediatrics. He had that rare gift of a good touch with his young patients plus excellent academic ability. Sharon's talents were no less as a nurse and midwife. She sensed how her mothers-to-be felt, and those insights helped her avoid the dramas some midwives experienced frequently.

It was like a bombshell to Drew's consultant that he was leaving. 'You're going to give all this up to go to some God-forsaken place and treat who knows what there?'

Drew resisted the temptation to say he aimed to make somewhere less God-forsaken. 'It's what's right for me. My calling.'

'Your calling? Aren't these poor sick kids you see every day your calling too? Don't *they* need a doctor?'

'There are plenty of doctors here to treat them. There are almost no doctors where I'll be going.'

But nothing could persuade the consultant. Eventually came the threat. 'You're twenty-eight and on the brink of a brilliant career in paediatrics. Opt out now and you kiss it all goodbye. If you leave, even for a few years, there's no way back. Others will overtake you and your commitment to your career will always be in doubt. Stay and I'll help you reach the top. Leave and you'll never make a consultancy.'

Drew came away from that meeting with a heavy heart. Being the best he could be was part of his nature. Climbing to the top of the ladder had been his ambition since before his studies began. To let it go was to shatter his dreams and his parents' too.

But there was no real choice. If it came down to being a medical supremo for his own fame and fortune or obeying God's call and helping the helpless, he knew what to do. Drew and Sharon became medical missionaries. And they've had no regrets.

Family

No-one expected Pat to be converted. She was too sophisticated and cynical to believe in God, too much of a party-goer and flirt to change her ways. But underneath the extrovert fun-loving exterior was a sensitive, questioning person. By the time she was twenty-one she knew there had to be more to life, something satisfying, something that lasted.

Friends at teacher training college told Pat about Jesus. They were afraid she'd mock. She didn't. She asked questions, read a book about Christianity, and asked some more questions. A month later she appeared in college with a big smile on her face. 'I've asked Jesus into my life,' she told her Christian friends. They laughed and cried together so much everyone thought them mad.

Pat bounced into her new faith with the enthusiasm she brought to everything. Within two days everyone she knew at college had heard about her conversion. Within a week virtually everyone else had too. Even the lecturers got told. She read her Bible from cover to cover, stayed up late to pray, joined the church, began teaching Sunday School and enrolled on a mission team to spend her summer telling people about Jesus. Pat's discipleship was a hundred and ten per cent. The changes in her life were radical.

She decided her parents had to know. She'd always been close to her mother, so she'd tell her what a difference Jesus had made. The chance came one Saturday afternoon when they were having coffee together at the kitchen table. Perhaps with more boldness than wisdom, she decided to hold nothing back. In graphic detail she told her mother what she'd done before becoming a Christian, the parties, the drinking, the boys and the sex.

When Pat finished there was silence. Finally Pat said softly, 'That's what I used to be like.'

Her mother put down her cup of coffee, and in a sad tone said, 'I wish you were still.'

It was a hard response from a mother who feared her daughter was becoming strange because she took Christianity seriously. She just wanted her to be normal, like everyone else, doing the crazy and bad things young people usually do.

Pat came to terms with what her mother said, but it hurt. It wasn't the reaction she'd wanted. The tough part was that she never really felt able to be honest with her mother again, never sure she could tell her how she felt or what she wanted to do with her life. In some way she felt rejected, that the person she'd become wasn't acceptable to her parents. There was a distance between them that had never been there before. She paid a high price for telling how God had changed her.

Facing risks

Driving in Asia has to be one of life's richest experiences. It's living to enjoy the riches which is doubtful. I heard a radio commentator, chatting between overs in a cricket match from Faisalabad in Pakistan, describe it well: 'You're in a beat-up taxi with a driver who puts the pedal flat to the floor, and careers along pot-holed roads that could shake the car to bits any moment. Then he decides to overtake the lorry in front. Somehow he squeezes more speed from the taxi, out he goes wide to get past, and there – coming straight for you – is a huge tanker. The blood drains from your face. Your driver doesn't flinch. The tanker is hurtling towards you and you towards it. There isn't room to squeeze between the lorry alongside and the tanker coming at you. You're about to die. The last second comes, and your driver hauls the steering wheel over and out you go even wider to the far verge, the tanker rushes between you and the lorry, and then calmly the taxi driver steers you back on to the road to complete your overtake.'

I believe that. I've been in a taxi in Faisalabad.

Virtually every missionary has a long list of near-death experiences to recite. The bus whose wheels went over the edge on a mountain pass. The cow that walked right in front of the motor-bike. The auto rickshaw that was crushed by the lorry. The over-laden bus that threw its passengers off the roof. These stories don't all have happy endings. Many get injured, and that's doubly serious in countries where there aren't emergency services to rush to your aid or hospitals you'd let treat your injuries. Not only do people get hurt, some die. Once I'd seen the risks missionaries took every time they went on the roads prayers for their safety shot way up the priority list.

Risks are not just from accidents. The danger can be disease. Even with modern medicines, mission workers get ill and some die. Malaria is still a great killer. The danger can be from crime. Brenda was alone in her house in an African country, when she was wakened in the night by a strange noise. Within seconds she realised she was being burgled. She hid behind her door, but knew that in two minutes she'd be found because the intruder was moving systematically from room to room. She was in extreme danger. Maybe she'd be raped. Even without that, very probably she'd be killed, for theft was less serious than being caught doing it. Her intruder would make sure she'd never tell. Brenda hurried to the window, hauled it open and climbed out. Across the compound she crept, pulled open the garage door and slipped inside. Somehow the burglar never looked there. He took what he wanted and left. If he hadn't Brenda could well have died.

Christine was travelling in an overnight train in an Asian country, and heard her compartment door being tried. A rough laugh outside told her there was an ambitious male wanting to get in. Though the door was locked, the fittings were ancient and they might break. She spoke his language, and told him to go away. That just made him angry. Next second Christine found herself staring down the barrel of a gun, pointed through a hole in the door. The man outside was a soldier. Christine shouted louder. The man laughed. In that country a woman couldn't expect help, and who would defend her from a soldier? The gun was swept around in a circle as Christine tried to get out of the firing line. Suddenly the gun was removed, the soldier moved away and it was as if nothing had ever happened. The only sound was the click-clack of train wheels on track. Christine lay down, but she didn't sleep again on that journey.

Margaret was manager of a hospital in another Asian country. Some locals didn't like having a Christian hospital in their area. They spread untrue stories that people had to go through forced conversions or they didn't get treated. Staff were threatened, and there were rumours the hospital would be burned down. Armed guards had to be stationed at the gate of the hospital day and night, and Margaret was advised never to go out alone. She was visited by the local chief of police. He offered her protection. Margaret was surprised. Of course, he explained, for the protection she'd have to make him a personal payment. She could hand over money or have sex with him. Margaret refused. From that day on Margaret knew that at best she'd get no protection from him and at worst she'd just gained another source of danger.

All these stories are true. And there could be dozens more, not just about single women, though they are in special danger. Some people would say, 'If it's as risky as that, why stay there?' There are three answers. First, to some extent they learn to cope. Risk is a way of life. Second, they know God has called them there and unless that call changes they can't leave. Third, there are millions of needy people in these places, people whom God loves and they want to get alongside. To run from risk is to run from these people. And they can't do that.

Antagonism
Of all student summer vacation jobs I had, this one was the most boring and badly organised. It was two months after a national census and I was employed to work in an immense warehouse where the completed forms were being processed. There were literally millions and millions of them in file boxes stacked row after row on roof-high racks. Some people had the brain-numbing job of sitting at tables writing computer codes against answers on the form so that they could eventually be entered into some huge and crude number cruncher. I had the brain- and body-numbing job of bringing the forms to these people and putting them back when they'd finished. That's all. Not exactly exciting.

What made a bad scene worse was that the set-up was a managerial disaster zone. Virtually every employee in the warehouse was temporary, including most of the supervisors. Many were students and the rest were on short-term contracts. Everyone had a vested interest in the work lasting as long as possible. No-one hurried anywhere. No-one searched for the quick way to get anything done. A supervisor called me over, and said, 'Fetch files J3R125 to J3R150 for the coders and, by the way, bring them one by one. Don't use a trolley. That would be too quick.' I couldn't believe he said that, but he did. And he meant it.

I was coping with working there only by imagining I was in

heaven keeping God's personal files about everyone on earth. The intrigue about what might be in those files brightened many a dull moment. But that mind-game triggered my conscience. If in any sense I was working for God rather than merely for the government, I had to do things in a way that pleased him. The go-slow policy most followed certainly didn't. I couldn't control what others did, but I could be in charge of my own work standard. So I began to go at a reasonable pace. I didn't run around, but I wasn't deliberately inefficient. I used trolleys. I brought files immediately. I tidied up. I asked for extra work when I'd nothing to do. Next day two fellows found me right in the middle of the tall racks, in a place no-one else could see or hear us. They came at me from either side. One grabbed my sweater in a tight fist, pushed me against the racks and muttered darkly, 'You can work as you so-and-so like, but you're not going to spoil things for us. Back off!' With a few more less than charming words they finished, let me go and disappeared. I gathered myself together, heaved a huge sigh, breathed a quick prayer, and got on with my work. For the several more weeks that job lasted I felt nervous every time I had to go deep among the racks. Would they be there again? What would they say? What would they do? I had to live with that. But I could. What I couldn't have lived with was not working rightly.

Any kind of witness for God draws antagonism. Some see that in terms of spiritual warfare. The devil will do anything to daunt or destroy God's servants. Some see it simply as opposition towards people who live differently, especially if they're showing up the poor standards of others. Whichever, the hostility is real.

Embarrassment

It was Monday morning but a good one. At least Al reckoned it was. The sun was shining, birds were singing and the spring blossom on the trees looked fabulous. But it wasn't just the joys of spring that made Al feel good. Truth was, the previous day had been the best Sunday of his Christian life. He'd been baptised during the morning service, with his family and friends there praying for him and encouraging him. The service had been deeply moving for Al, with a remarkable sense of God's presence. He hadn't been the only one to feel that, and it had thrilled his heart when his friend Andy made a first-time commitment to Jesus at the end of the service. The evening hadn't been nearly so outwardly dramatic, but he'd listened to a sermon that touched his heart and made him feel God was speaking personally to him. It was too soon to know how important that would be, but it had been a great experience.

So he was going into a new week on a spiritual high. God was real, Jesus was alive, and the Spirit was with him. Life was good. Into the office Al breezed. 'Good morning!' he said enthusiastically to Mary, one of the typists.

She smiled. 'So what are you so happy about this morning?'

Words got right to the tip of Al's tongue, words about how great it was to be a Christian and how God meant so much to him. The words of witness were right there to speak out. But Al was hit right that moment with an embarrassment seizure. To talk about God was fine in church, but to say anything about God in that office would seem so strange. Mary was waiting. 'Well . . . it's a lovely morning . . . isn't it?' he stammered lamely, and slunk away to his desk. He'd missed his moment to witness and felt a failure. Embarrassment had won over mission.

Of course, that Al is really Alistair, for that was me the day after my baptism, descending fast spiritually from mountain peak to valley floor. I tell that as the final story in a chapter on how mission is hard, sometimes so hard we fail.

Sometimes threats are so great we run. That isn't always wrong. When Paul and his companions were persecuted, sometimes they stayed and accepted whatever harsh treatment came their way including being beaten or flogged. But sometimes they left, able to move on alive to another town and carry on the mission there. One time it was right to stay; another time it was right to go.

But usually backing down on witness is wrong. Even though it costs, we're meant to take opportunities, not miss them. The goal is winning the lost, not guarding our image and not even protecting our years on this earth. We're supposed to be dead to self, our old natures crucified. Crucified those old natures may be, but they can have a remarkable life after death. All too often we choke on our words when we should speak them. We're passive when we should be active. We're absent when we should be present. Paul could boast that he was not ashamed of the gospel. We often are.

We fail, but we're not failures. God loves us still, and when we fall God's only desire is that we get up, admit our weakness, accept his forgiveness and then get on with living and witnessing as we should. There are two temptations. One is to beat ourselves up. 'I'm no good.' The other is to write ourselves off. 'I'll never be able to witness for God.' We fail, but the Father still accepts us as his children, and still uses us in the future. We're not written out of his family and not written out of his plans.

Mission is hard. There's a rough old world out there which isn't waiting with welcoming arms for Christians to bring it the gospel. Mission aims to do people good. They ought to be grateful but often they're hostile. God protects, but that doesn't mean nothing bad can happen to us. Mission isn't for the faint-hearted. Mission can hurt. But even if sometimes we back off, God recalls us. And through weak people like us God gets great things done in the world.

Chapter 4

The only hope

An old legend

Jesus leaves his disciples on earth and returns to heaven in triumph to be greeted by a thronging crowd of angels. Michael, Gabriel and the rest are all there, applauding him home, celebrating his great victory over sin, death and hell, bringing mankind forgiveness of sins.

When the hubbub settles, one of the angels asks, 'Now, Lord, how many legions of the heavenly hosts do you need so that this gospel can be told to all people?'

'None,' replied Jesus.

'But everyone must know. Everyone must hear the way of salvation.'

'I have left twelve men behind, and given them that work.'

'Twelve? Men? Lord, men are so feeble and likely to fail. What if they do? What then?'

'Then there is no other plan. Just them.'

WHEN HE WAS four my son went missing. Alison, my wife, had me called home from a deacons' meeting. Before long we had all the deacons out looking along with us for my youngster who had disappeared. Street after street we combed, looking in every doorway and every garden. While others then checked the local woods and pond, I searched the school playground. None of us found him. In the end he strolled back home. He'd walked for a few miles, seen enough of the world to satisfy his curiosity for the moment, and come home for his supper. If he hadn't I'd have gone on looking all night. My son was lost; at age four he was at risk out on his own. I was very motivated to find him.

God is very motivated to find his lost children. And he has no strategy to speak to the world he loves except through Christians. He won't be sending out legions of angels; he won't be shouting at sinners via loudspeakers pointed through the clouds; he isn't writing John 3:16 across the sky; he isn't dropping tracts like confetti; he isn't beaming down any other saviours to earth. He's sent Jesus, and through those who have found faith in him he plans that others will come to faith.

If that's true – the only hope this world has is Jesus, and the only way people can discover Jesus is through us – our part in mission becomes critically important.

I don't like that thought. I'm scared that anyone's eternity would be dependent on me, even a little bit dependent on me. I'd rather avoid that responsibility, partly so I can make choices free of obligation, and partly because I'm terrified I'll fail. I wouldn't like to pack parachutes for a living because I couldn't cope with knowing that if I didn't do my work properly someone would die. Likewise I don't want to think anyone's eternity rests on me telling them about Jesus.

But it does have something to do with it. God has no other plan than using us. Several basic blocks of biblical teaching build that conclusion.

Alienation from God

The Bible opens with scenes of man and God in a wonderful relationship of honesty, harmony and friendship. There's a genuine closeness. That's not how it is now. People today are distant from God. God and man have split up. We understand ordinary break-ups between people. Almost every family seems to have at least one major rift. Maybe a marriage has gone on the rocks. Joe and Mabel have always had a stormy time, but Joe was visiting Agnes next door more often than he was at home and Mabel has thrown him out. Or the family bust-up is of a different kind. Once too often Ethel shared her wisdom on how children need discipline, and how

Surely the arm of the LORD is not too short to save,
    nor his ear too dull to hear.
But your iniquities have separated
    you from your God;
your sins have hidden his face from you,
    so that he will not hear.
For your hands are stained with blood,
    your fingers with guilt.
Your lips have spoken lies,
    and your tongue mutters wicked things.
So justice is far from us,
    and righteousness does not reach us.
We look for light, but all is darkness;
    for brightness, but we walk in deep shadows.
Like the blind we grope along the wall,
    feeling our way like men without eyes.
At midday we stumble as if it were twilight;
    among the strong, we are like the dead.
We all growl like bears;
    we moan mournfully like doves.
We look for justice, but find none;
    for deliverance, but it is far away.
For our offences are many in your sight,
    and our sins testify against us.
Our offences are ever with us,
    and we acknowledge our iniquities:
rebellion and treachery against the LORD,
    turning our backs on our God,
fomenting oppression and revolt,
    uttering lies our hearts have conceived.

Isa. 59:1–3, 9–13

she'd make a much better job of raising them than her sisters are doing. Now Ethel doesn't get invited even to funerals. Separations something like these are commonplace today. Whose fault is humankind's separation from God? Is it anyone's? Some breaks are just misunderstandings, or the blame is on both sides. Not this one. There's nothing accidental or both-sided about the estrangement between man and God. The Bible is clear that it's our wrongdoing that's caused the alienation. As Isaiah puts it, we're guilty of 'turning our backs on our God' and, because we've betrayed someone who has faithfully loved us, it amounts to 'rebellion and treachery' (Isa. 59:13).

That's no small thing. Rebellion isn't minor, something God might shrug off. Nor is God puny, a wimp unable to stand up to those abusing him. He is the holy and almighty Lord of all who will not turn a blind eye to those who go to war against his rulership. Isaiah prophesies judgment. Humankind will get what is due for being at war with God.

> According to what they have done,
>   so will he repay
> wrath to his enemies
>   and retribution to his foes;
>   he will repay the islands their due.
>
> Isa. 59:18

Judgment is not merely an Old Testament understanding of how God works. The New Testament is equally sure that those who live against God are judged.

Jesus was clear that there would be a reckoning for all. He said: 'I tell you that men will have to give account on the day of judgment for every careless word they have spoken' (Matt. 12:36). He told several lengthy parables about times of reckoning. Servants gave account for how they'd invested 'talents' put in their charge. 'Sheep' and 'goats' were judged for their care for the disadvantaged around them. Everyone should be ready for their lives to undergo God's scrutiny:

Who then is the faithful and wise servant, whom the master has put in charge of the servants in his household to give them their food at the proper time? It will be good for that servant whose master finds him doing so when he returns. I tell you the truth, he will put him in charge of all his possessions. But suppose that servant is wicked and says to himself, 'My master is staying away a long time,' and he then begins to beat his fellow-servants and to eat and drink with drunkards. The master of that servant will come on a day when he does not expect him and at an hour he is not aware of. He will cut him to pieces and assign him a place with the hypocrites, where there will be weeping and gnashing of teeth. (Matt. 24:45–51)

Paul talked of God's wrath falling on those who live against God. Two themes stand out clearly from Paul's words. a) Judgment will be fair. It'll be 'righteous', based on what each has or has not done. God will not make mistakes. b) Judgment will be for all, for 'each person', for 'every human being'. As he puts it later, the whole world will be held accountable to God (Rom. 3:19). No-one will escape.

But because of your stubbornness and your unrepentant heart, you are storing up wrath against yourself for the day of God's wrath, when his righteous judgment will be revealed. God 'will give to each person according to what he has done'. To those who by persistence in doing good seek glory, honour and immortality, he will give eternal life. But for those who are self-seeking and who reject the truth and follow evil, there will be wrath and anger. There will be trouble and distress for every human being who does evil.
Rom. 2:5–9

So, people live distant from God. They're alienated and that alienation is earning them judgment.

Hell

My Mum was a great Christian, but not at all sure about the existence of hell. 'I just don't like the thought of it,' she once told me. Plenty are like her. To some extent, most of us shape our theology according to what we'd like to be true. Hell is distasteful. When faced with the possibility that much loved friends might go there, we're inclined to disinvent it. We don't want such a terrible eternal destiny to exist. But what we want or don't want doesn't determine what really is.

I don't know what hell is, but I know what it's not. It's not being with God and it's not experiencing the blessings God gives: love, kindness, mercy, goodness. Take away all the positive things that God provides: rain to water the earth; a bird that sings its tune; the smile of a little child; the hug of a friend; an act of kindness to a lonely old person; healing for a hurting body; forgiveness of past wrongs; strength to face a new day; hope for a better future; and much more. Life already feels 'hellish' if we miss out on even one of these. But suppose they were all gone? What would be left is unspeakably bad and terrifying. Only pain, only deprivation, only cruelty, only evil, only weakness, only regret, only despair. I'm sure the depth of the sadness and horror is more than my mind can grasp.

> Once again, the kingdom of heaven is like a net that was let down into the lake and caught all kinds of fish. When it was full, the fishermen pulled it up on the shore. Then they sat down and collected the good fish in baskets, but threw the bad away. This is how it will be at the end of the age. The angels will come and separate the wicked from the righteous and throw them into the fiery furnace, where there will be weeping and gnashing of teeth.
>
> Matt. 13:47–50

That's undoubtedly why Jesus used dramatic imagery – vivid pictures such as a fiery furnace – to give us some idea of what hell is like. There will always be those who want to debate if these words are meant literally, whether angels will actually stand by a fiery furnace and throw sinners in. But the debates are pointless. For one thing, Jesus had to use analogies and metaphors. They were unavoidable. The only way to describe something beyond someone's range of knowledge and experience is to say it's like something which is familiar. What will happen in eternity is unimaginable to our finite minds. Jesus had to use known things as analogies. Besides, the essential point Jesus wanted us to know is perfectly plain: to be found out of favour with God come judgment day is an appalling prospect. The dreadful imagery reflects a dreadful reality. Hell is a destiny no-one could want. Better to cut off hands and feet or pluck out eyes than go there, according to Jesus. Any sacrifice would be worth it to avoid hell.

> And if anyone causes one of these little ones who believe in me to sin, it would be better for him to be thrown into the sea with a large millstone tied around his neck. If your hand causes you to sin, cut it off. It is better for you to enter life maimed than with two hands to go into hell, where the fire never goes out. And if your foot causes you to sin, cut it off. It is better for you to enter life crippled than to have two feet and be thrown into hell. And if your eye causes you to sin, pluck it out. It is better for you to enter the kingdom of God with one eye than to have two eyes and be thrown into hell, where
> 'their worm does not die,
> and the fire is not quenched.'
>
> Mark 9:42–8

Whatever hell is exactly, it's not a good place to be. There's nothing positive, nothing to be desired, nothing pleasing about hell. To be where God is not is a terrifying eternity. Jesus could not have spoken more strongly about it.

Escape

No-one has lived a perfect life. No-one has achieved a standard that would entitle them to be in heaven. 'For all have sinned and fall short of the glory of God' (Rom. 3:23). If all are to be judged and judgment leads to hell, the logical conclusion is that heaven stays empty and hell is fully populated.

The gospel is all about escaping that logic. It's about judgment falling, but not on us. One of my favourite illustrations of that is the story of two duck hunters. They're searching dry scrubland when they sniff fire in the air. The bushes in the distance are alight and, to their horror, they realise the wind is blowing a wall of fire in their direction. Crashing madly through the undergrowth, they try to outrun the flames. But it's hopeless. The ground is tinder-dry and the fire is spreading at virtually the speed of the wind. They'll never escape. All seems lost. But one of them has an idea.

He tells his friend to stand clear, takes out his lighter, and sets the scrub on fire near where they're standing. In an instant it blazes as the dry grass is consumed. In seconds an area some ten metres square is blackened earth. Just as the advancing wall of flame reaches them, the duck hunters throw themselves on the patch of blackened earth. All around them is fire; the heat is intense. But, as the flames move on, the men rise unscathed. The fire had already burned where they lay, and it couldn't burn there again. So they lived.

Whoever believes in the Son has eternal life, but whoever rejects the Son will not see life, for God's wrath remains on him. John 3:36

Jesus answered, 'I am the way and the truth and the life. No-one comes to the Father except through me.' John 14:6

Salvation is found in no-one else, for there is no other name under heaven given to men by which we must be saved. Acts 4:12

Jesus is like that blackened earth. He took our sin. God's wrath at our failure and rebellion fell on him. Those who 'throw themselves' on Jesus find the one place of safety, the one place God's judgment has fallen already, and so they live. That makes Jesus very special. There are no other saviours or mediators between man and God, no other religion and no other way for people to get back to God. No-one will ever be good enough for a perfectly holy God; no-one can offer a bribe to the one who is already Lord of all; no-one will persuade a just God to set aside his own moral laws and ignore sin. All any of us can do is be humble. We acknowledge our guilt, accept that Jesus's death on the cross was in our place, and identify ourselves wholly with him.

Jesus, then, is unique. He is the one and only Saviour for all people. That's not to say there's nothing good or nothing of truth in religions or philosophies that don't prioritise Jesus. They may point people in the right direction. They may show something of what God is like. But they don't reveal God perfectly like Jesus did. They don't provide a Saviour who has died in place of us. They don't map out the way through death to resurrection like Jesus. There is no-one like Jesus. 'For there is one God and one mediator between God and men, the man Christ Jesus, who gave himself as a ransom for all men' (1 Tim. 2:5–6).

The one way

A small island lies just off the coast. The island has sheer rock sides, and there's no access by boat. The only way on to it is by the one bridge which links it to the shore. It's a narrow rope bridge, high above sharp rocks. It swings in the wind, and only the bravest dare use it, for one step the wrong way would be to destruction. Many who would like to cross haven't the courage. There are other paths or roads in the area. They're broader, easier, less risky. People use them to get a view of the island's rugged beauty. But those who want actually to reach the island have to take the risk of that one bridge.

Jesus is the one way out of alienation and back into a relationship of peace with God. 'Therefore, there is now no condemnation for those who are in Christ Jesus, because through Christ Jesus the law of the Spirit of life set me free from the law of sin and death' (Rom. 8:1–2).

Opportunities

Paul told the Romans, 'If you confess with your mouth, "Jesus is Lord," and believe in your heart that God raised him from the dead, you will be saved' (10:9). That's what's possible. He quoted Joel, 'Everyone who calls on the name of the Lord will be saved' (10:13). Possible, yes, but available? The two are not necessarily the same, as everyone who has ever proposed marriage and been given a negative reply can testify.

Using four questions (Rom. 10:14–15), Paul asks about the availability of salvation. He starts from the need to call on Jesus, and moves backward in logic to show why they can't do that:

- How, then, can they call on the one they have not believed in?
- And how can they believe in the one of whom they have not heard?
- And how can they hear without someone preaching to them?
- And how can they preach unless they are sent?

Here are Paul's four questions put in other words:

- People should call on Jesus to save them, but if they don't believe in him – that he's God's Son who died in their place – why would they?
- They'll never believe in him if they don't even know he exists.
- They'll never know he exists unless someone tells them.
- No-one will tell them unless they go to them.

Putting it very simply: you won't believe without a reason; you've no reason to believe what you don't know; you can't know unless someone tells you; no-one will tell you unless they're in touch with you.

Picture a crew of blind canoeists paddling downstream towards Niagara, unaware the falls are just ahead. Their trip is exhilarating. The water is flowing fast. They like that; there's the thrill of rapid movement and it makes their work easier. There's a distant sound of roaring. It means nothing to them; it could be the engines of the nearby power station. On and on they paddle, innocently and ignorantly heading for destruction. At that point escape is still possible. They're not so far down or gripped by the current that they couldn't turn. But they won't turn, not because they want to die, but because they don't know they need to turn. And they'll never know before it's too late unless someone on the bank who sees their danger shouts a warning loud enough for them to hear, or gets into a powerboat and motors out to them. Only if someone intervenes, only if someone tells, will those blind canoeists know they must change course.

Paul saw an urgency about mission like that. He felt a compulsion to make Jesus known where he wasn't known. He moved from place to place, sometimes staying for a time to teach converts, sometimes moving on quickly to other towns. Often he was persecuted. Sometimes he almost died. But the message had to get out. It was important – life-changing – and people must be told. Salvation was possible, but not available unless people knew about Jesus. Only then did they have the chance to believe and be saved.

None lost?

Is that last section true? Are people heading for a lost eternity unless they're told of Jesus and believe in him? Jesus may have said, 'I am the way and the truth and the life. No-one comes to the Father except through me' (John 14:6), but was he right? Or have we misunderstood him?

The other day I heard someone say that no-one will be lost because God will press home his love to people over and over until they are bound to yield to it. God is patient and persistent. He won't ever give up. Though people may reject him and reject the gospel, he will never abandon them, never give up on them. No matter how long it takes he will go on showing mercy until they finally accept and respond to him. Thus all will be saved. He didn't explain what happened if time ran out in this life before they believed, for, as far as can be known, many have died still vehemently opposing God. Were they to move on into some form of purgatory to get a time for fresh thinking? Nevertheless, his main point is that the fact that God loves all means he'll make sure all go to heaven.

Twenty years ago, I debated the same issue with some fellow-students in a philosophy of religion class. Five argued that a God of love couldn't send anyone to hell. His love obliged him to take them to heaven. I argued that precisely because he is a God of love he can't force people into heaven who haven't chosen to go there.

The comics I read as a youngster frequently had variations of one cartoon strip. It showed Caveman Fred setting off to find a wife, wearing his best animal skin and with a huge club in his hand. Over hill and through valley he trudged, surveying the female population. Finally Fred found a woman suitably attractive and looking capable of hard work. Bop! One hard bump on the head with the club, she was knocked out, and Caveman Fred could drag her back to his cave to make her his wife. Fred's method was efficient. (In my late teens I wished it still existed – far easier than all the mysterious and emotional business of boy–girl relationships.) Simple and effective it may have been but it was never love. Fred's wife never had the chance to say 'no'. Love doesn't do that. Love never compels against a person's will.

God so loves us that he allows us the freedom to accept or refuse his love, his gospel, his Son. God has immense respect for us. He creates us with the ability to make choices, and he so respects us that he honours these choices, even bad ones. Certainly he persists in putting his love to us many times. We don't get just one chance and if we miss that moment there's never another. But if throughout this life we refuse, God treats us as the responsible people we are and accepts our choice. He grants us the eternity for which we've opted, an eternity without him. To force someone into heaven would be a form of spiritual rape.

What of those who've never heard of Jesus? They haven't deliberately rejected him. They've never had the chance to accept. Are they lost? That's a hugely difficult question. Any answers are too simplistic, but these points need to be kept in mind.

1. Ignorance is rarely bliss.
2. The Bible never suggests there are two ways of getting to heaven, one by knowing Jesus and the other by knowing nothing about Jesus. If the latter were true, it would have been better for Jesus to have *banned* evangelism, not commissioned it.
3. The apostles started from the position of virtually no-one else knowing about Jesus. They clearly considered that others needed to know, hence they preached everywhere even if it meant great danger for them.
4. Paul's commissioning to take the gospel to the Gentiles was because they *had* to hear: 'I have appeared to you to appoint you as a servant and as a witness of what you have seen of me and what I will show you. I will rescue you from your own people and from the Gentiles. I am sending you to them to open their eyes and turn them from darkness to light, and from the power of Satan to God, so that they may receive forgiveness of sins and a place among those who are sanctified by faith in me' (Acts 26:16–18).
5. God is just and merciful, and will never give anyone a wrong judgment.
6. There's a glimmer in a few places in the Bible, like Romans 1, that

people will be judged on the basis of the response they make to the revelation they've had. Some know nothing of Jesus, but understand something of God in other ways such as through creation. Maybe the way they've reacted to the little they know of God will be their judgment. The down-side is that people tend to reject God, not submit to him.

> What may be known about God is plain to them, because God has made it plain to them. For since the creation of the world God's invisible qualities – his eternal power and divine nature – have been clearly seen, being understood from what has been made, so that men are without excuse.
> For although they knew God, they neither glorified him as God nor gave thanks to him, but their thinking became futile and their foolish hearts were darkened.
>
> Rom. 1:19–21

The overwhelming balance of the Bible's teaching is that people need to have faith in Jesus to have a future in heaven. God wants everyone in heaven. He has no desire to condemn anyone. When I was twelve I had a schoolteacher who seemed to enjoy belting his pupils. I remember one lad whose unjustified absence from school got him a belting so hard he literally jumped around with pain in front of the whole class. That teacher seemed to take sadistic pleasure in punishing people. God is no sadist. He has no desire to hurt. His heart breaks for his lost children. So out of love he has sent a rescuer. Those willing to be rescued by him get a new life and a new eternity. Those who refuse rescue sentence themselves to the judgment that follows from opposing the God who should be honoured as Lord.

Billy Graham's book *Approaching Hoofbeats* begins with the story of Harry Truman. He lived five miles north of Mt Saint Helens in Washington. In 1980 the mountain began to belch plumes of dark smoke. Scientists ran innumerable tests and issued the alert: the mountain was about to erupt. Everything swung into place. Signs were put up at road ends; police helicopters blared warnings; TV and radio broadcasts gave updates. Everyone moved. Except Harry. Rangers, neighbours, his sister begged him. He just

> For God so loved the world that he gave his one and only Son, that whoever believes in him shall not perish but have eternal life. For God did not send his Son into the world to condemn the world, but to save the world through him. Whoever believes in him is not condemned, but whoever does not believe stands condemned already because he has not believed in the name of God's one and only Son.
>
> John 3:16–18

grinned. 'Nobody knows more about this mountain than Harry and it don't dare blow up on him . . .' At 8.31 a.m. on 18 May 1980 Harry Truman was destroyed with the mountain as 150 square miles of landscape disintegrated in a massive explosion that sent a cloud ten miles into the sky. Harry had the chance to live. But he wouldn't take it.

God's longing for all to be saved couldn't be clearer but only those who take the chance offered through Jesus will live.

Motivated for mission

This is a lost world, and it's at great risk. Alienated from God and facing judgment; liable to a hell terrible beyond comprehension. Yet with a Saviour come, one who died to remove judgment and hell from mankind. Now it's possible for all to find a new life, new freedom, new destiny. Faced with that, I want every single person in the world to know that possibility. This beggar knows where there's food, and wants every other hungry beggar to know where it is too, for there's enough for all.

If I really care for the lost world, I'll have a sense of motivation, urgency and determination to make sure every man, woman and child gets to hear of Jesus. They *must* hear. It's vitally important. And like it or not, whether they hear depends on us. Do I really believe people are spiritually lost to God? Do I really believe people will spend eternity without God? Do I really believe Jesus died for every one of them? Do I really believe they can have eternal life only if they get to hear about Jesus and believe in him? Do I really believe these people have as much worth as I do?

I ask those questions forcefully of myself, for the answers to what I really believe aren't any theories I write in this book. The answers to what I really believe are shown by what I do. Do I speak up about Jesus or keep quiet? Do I use my time, my money, my career for myself or others? Do I set aside my own wants if that helps make Jesus known?

God had given me far more than was sufficient to keep my body and soul together, and, I thought, how could I spend the best years of my life in working for myself and the honours and pleasures of this world, while thousands and thousands of souls are perishing every day without having heard of Christ?

C. T. Studd, Cricketer and Pioneer, Norman P. Grubb
(The Religious Tract Society, 1933)

My choices – the ones I make every day and the long-term choices that set the pattern for my way of life – show what I really believe. God alone is my judge, but I hope the choices I'm making show that I do believe people are lost and that I'm willing to give my life to helping them be found again. Jesus is their only hope. If that's true, and it is; if I care for people, and I do; then I must be motivated about mission.

No other response is reasonable. Nothing less than sharing what I have seems human, never mind Christian. Suppose there was a shipwreck. The liner is sinking. You are thrown into the water, but find a huge lifeboat bobbing nearby and scramble into it. You're safe. But all around you people are drowning. If rescuing them overloaded your lifeboat and caused it to sink, perhaps doing nothing to help would be comprehensible. But this is a massive lifeboat. There's more than enough space for everyone. If you do nothing to save the people drowning that will be an act of grossest selfishness amounting to a terrible evil. You can't settle down, breathe a sigh of relief that you're all right and ignore their cries for help. To know they're dying but you can rescue them must drive you to throw out lifelines or grasp desperate hands and pull people to safety.

We have the gospel. We are children of God, confident that we've been rescued from our sins and we're heaven-bound. But others aren't. All around I hear cries for help. The woman betrayed by an unfaithful husband. The girl abused by a father who thinks only of his wants. The refugee desperate to feed his starving family. The wealthy businessman who knows he has everything this world can give but nothing of ultimate value. The devalued and rejected villager with no status in his society. The addict whose habit is destroying mind and body. The family terrorised by evil spirits who destroy their lives. The person who knows he's failed and wants to begin again. These, and others, are loud voices in the world today. I can't bask in the light and leave them to suffer and die in darkness.

In the end it all comes down to what I really believe.

The following words of William Ward, a missionary based at Serampore, India, sum it up. He was writing to converts in the Chittagong area in April 1818. His language is old-fashioned, of course, but what he believed is clear. A passion for mission is the only reasonable response to a lost world.

Consider, that all these your countrymen are dying and going to misery. Would you not save a man if he were drowning? Would you not awake a man if his house were on fire, and try to pull him out of the flames? How much more should you try to prevent your countrymen from falling into the unquenchable fire, where they will have to abide for ever! O then be not idle in this great work. Labour day and night, and beg of them with tears not to cast themselves into hell, but to come to Christ and live.

Chapter 5

Changing the world

IMAGINE A MINING disaster. Hundreds of feet below ground, the roof has caved in. Rocks have fallen, gas is seeping along what remains of tunnels, floodwater is gradually rising. Dozens are buried, with many feared dead. Yet it's known that at least some are still alive. Ambulances and rescue teams rush to the mine.

Let's press the pause button on this unfolding drama. What are the various people involved in the aftermath of this disaster trying to achieve? The number one goal must be to save those who are still alive. Next will be to bring comfort to those who are dying and their relatives. Is there more? An important goal is to learn lessons so that such a disaster won't happen again. Anything more? Yes, to restore the mine so that it can function as its owner intended.

So the rescue proceeds. The short-term goal is to get as many out alive as possible. The long-term goal is to make this mine safe for the future.

Mission is as comprehensive as that. It's not only plucking a few brands from the fire. It's working towards an answer to the prayer Jesus taught his disciples, to ask that the Father's kingdom should come, that his will should be done on earth as it is in heaven.

The prayer is for people to experience God's rulership. That can't be imposed. It's not for some zealots to pass laws requiring every citizen to acknowledge God and behave morally or be thrown into jail. Jesus could easily have made himself that kind of king, but clearly avoided it. His kingdom was not to be forced on people but would be one they willingly chose to enter. So, God's gift of freedom for mankind, sorely abused, remains. God's longing is for people to take his gift of love and respond with theirs, to accept his lordship joyfully and gratefully. That way they'll experience God's

Our Father in heaven,
hallowed be your name,
your kingdom come,
your will be done
    on earth as it is in heaven.
Give us today our daily bread.
Forgive us our debts,
    as we also have forgiven our debtors.
And lead us not into temptation,
but deliver us from the evil one.

Matt. 6:9–13

kingdom on earth as in heaven. Putting that invitation and challenge before them is mission.

He went to Nazareth, where he had been brought up, and on the Sabbath day he went into the synagogue, as was his custom. And he stood up to read. The scroll of the prophet Isaiah was handed to him. Unrolling it, he found the place where it is written:
    'The Spirit of the Lord is on me,
      because he has anointed me
      to preach good news to the poor.
    He has sent me to proclaim freedom for the prisoners
      and recovery of sight for the blind,
    to release the oppressed,
      to proclaim the year of the Lord's favour.'
Then he rolled up the scroll, gave it back to the attendant and sat down. The eyes of everyone in the synagogue were fastened on him, and he began by saying to them, 'Today this scripture is fulfilled in your hearing.'

Luke 4:16–21

Jesus began it. His words in the synagogue at Nazareth were not merely a quotation from the Old Testament. Nor were they to be taken only with some otherworldly spiritual meaning as if nothing would happen in this world and all would change in the next. Jesus was being short-term as well as long-term, dealing with the here and now as well as the there and then. This was his manifesto. These things were his agenda. Blind people like Bartimaeus would see. Oppressed people like the Gadarene demoniac would be released. For work like that, and for much more, Jesus had been anointed with the Spirit.

The mission to which we are called is that radical. It changes life on this earth. It regards this world as still belonging to God, a place for him to work and rule. It regards people as having value and being loved, with a need to have a broken relationship with God mended so they can share eternity with him. Mission, then, falls under three broad headings.

I. Helping individuals find salvation

One of the buzz terms I encounter almost every day is holistic mission. It means mission to the whole person. I like the phrase because I like that meaning. God made us body, mind and spirit. He doesn't have an interest in only part of us. Mission must deal with every facet of our being. We're called to make disciples, not hunt for spiritual scalps.

Sometimes, though, the term 'holistic mission' is used to mean everything except conversion. It's understanding culture, relieving hunger and poverty, defending against oppression, and plenty more like that. But it's not calling people to faith. It's not telling them to abandon false belief systems for a real relationship with God. It seems to suggest a distressed Paul on the road to Damascus needed a psychologist to help him with his guilt rather than an encounter with the risen Christ to bring him forgiveness. It's as if we should apologise to the sorcerers of Ephesus who made a public bonfire of their scrolls as they came to believe in Jesus because the Christians may have brainwashed them into accepting someone else's culture.

Mission to the whole person covers the need of the whole person, and that includes spiritual rebirth. That's new beliefs, new motivation, new lifestyle, new goals, new power. It's a profound change for every aspect of life. Without that, someone hasn't become a Christian. Jesus began his preaching ministry by commanding 'Repent and believe the good news!' (Mark 1:15) Those strong words weren't just to make an initial impact. It was a recurring theme:

- 'Unless you repent, you too will all perish' (Luke 13:3).
- 'I tell you that in the same way there will be more rejoicing in heaven over one sinner who repents than over ninety-nine righteous persons who do not need to repent' (Luke 15:7).

In reply Jesus declared, 'I tell you the truth, no-one can see the kingdom of God unless he is born again.'

'How can a man be born when he is old?' Nicodemus asked. 'Surely he cannot enter a second time into his mother's womb to be born!'

Jesus answered, 'I tell you the truth, no-one can enter the kingdom of God unless he is born of water and the Spirit.'

John 3:3–5

The same need for change comes through in Jesus's words to Nicodemus. The man was already very religious and spiritual. He believed in God, knew the Scriptures, taught others and led the nation. He was thoroughly religious, and he recognised Jesus was sent from God. But despite his pedigree and insights Jesus was still blunt with him, that there's no entry into the kingdom of God without a second birth.

Jesus wasn't the only one to call for people to experience a spiritual transformation. That was also the message of those who carried on his work.

- 'They went out and preached that people should repent' (Mark 6:12).
- 'Peter replied, "Repent and be baptised, every one of you, in the name of Jesus Christ for the forgiveness of your sins. And you will receive the gift of the Holy Spirit" ' (Acts 2:38).
- 'They replied, "Believe in the Lord Jesus, and you will be saved – you and your household" ' (Acts 16:31).
- 'In the past God overlooked such ignorance, but now he commands all people everywhere to repent' (Acts 17:30).
- 'If you confess with your mouth, "Jesus is Lord," and believe in your

heart that God raised him from the dead, you will be saved' (Rom. 10:9).

- 'Therefore, if anyone is in Christ, he is a new creation; the old has gone, the new has come!' (2 Cor. 5:17)

It was good that Mary Magdalene had demons driven from her, but that wasn't what saved her. Nor was Zacchaeus saved by learning to be honest about tax-collecting. Nor was Bartimaeus saved because his eyesight was restored. Getting rid of whatever forms of bondage, dishonesty and disability characterised their lives mattered. But those things didn't produce a new destiny for them. No matter how many outward changes happened in their lives those changes didn't make them heaven-bound. They needed their inner natures transformed.

Hence, for the early Christian preachers conversion wasn't an option. It was foundational. It was the change of nature and change of status that led to every other change in a disciple's life. 'Dear friends, now we are children of God . . . No-one who is born of God will continue to sin, because God's seed remains in him; he cannot go on sinning, because he has been born of God' (1 John 3:2, 9).

In essence, two things needed to be different in each person.

What they believed

There had to be new knowledge, a new perspective on Jesus. Ignorance wouldn't do. Nor was it enough to respect Jesus as a good man, wise teacher or powerful prophet. Jesus was much more: Messiah, Son of God, Saviour. He was someone to know as Lord, someone to trust for salvation.

The depth of knowledge shouldn't be overstated. For some it was partial and imperfect, perhaps seriously so. The dying thief on a cross next to Jesus understood little theology. There were no great doctrinal confessions from him. All he seems to have grasped was that Jesus was Lord of a new kingdom, one beyond this life, so he begged for a place in that kingdom. And he got it.

Believing is not fundamentally about having a certain amount of knowledge. Without realising it, often we've assumed there's a critical point when knowing and believing enough truths about

Jesus make someone a Christian. It's as if there's a sliding scale: 0 equals no knowledge or belief; 10 equals the deepest and best of these that anyone can have. We progress out of ignorance, past 1, 2 and maybe 3 and when we reach about 4 or 5 we know enough about Jesus – we understand who he is and what he has done – so we're considered Christian.

On that basis Judas Iscariot should have been a strong Christian. He heard Jesus's teaching, saw his miracles, shared his company. His first-hand experience and understanding ought to have made him more of a Christian than anyone today. But he wasn't.

The critical need is not belief in the sense of knowledge but belief in the sense of trust. Here are two statements. 1) 'I believe Harry Higglesworth is a rich financier'; 2) 'I believe Harry Higglesworth is a rich financier, and because I also know he's honest and hard-working I'm willing to invest my life savings in his company.' The first says what I know; the second says that on the basis of all I know I'm willing to trust Harry. The latter is believing in the biblical sense. The belief may be of only mustard-seed quantity – it might score only 1 out of 10 on the sliding scale – but it inspires trust.

What people believed – in the sense of what they were committed to – needed to change.

What they did
Converts are changed people, not just in their thinking, but in their way of life.

> What good is it, my brothers, if a man claims to have faith but has no deeds? Can such faith save him? Suppose a brother or sister is without clothes and daily food. If one of you says to him, 'Go, I wish you well; keep warm and well fed,' but does nothing about his physical needs, what good is it? In the same way, faith by itself, if it is not accompanied by action, is dead.
>
> James 2:14–17

Some say the only thing that matters is having faith. James specifically says it's not, at least not if the definition of having faith excludes the way someone lives. The faith Christians have must change them. The caterpillar spins a cocoon around itself. When it emerges it isn't still a caterpillar. It's a butterfly. Now it soars over the flowers instead of crawling over the earth. Christians have also been through a metamorphosis. The way they behave, how they treat others, the things that drive them, all are different from before.

> Therefore everyone who hears these words of mine and puts them into practice is like a wise man who built his house on the rock. The rain came down, the streams rose, and the winds blew and beat against that house; yet it did not fall, because it had its foundation on the rock. But everyone who hears these words of mine and does not put them into practice is like a foolish man who built his house on sand. The rain came down, the streams rose, and the winds blew and beat against that house, and it fell with a great crash.
>
> Matt. 7:24–7

I was deceived at Sunday School. Whether it was the words of the song or the way the story was told, I grew up misunderstanding Jesus's analogy about the two men who built houses, one on rock and the other on sand. When the rain fell, streams rose, and winds blew, the house on the rock stood because it had a solid foundation but the house on the sand fell because it was based on shifting sand. I loved the story. It was with the application that I was misguided. I was told the first man represented the wise person who believed in Jesus and the second man represented the foolish person who didn't. But that's not what Jesus said. The first was the person who hears his words and does them, and the second the person who hears his words and ignores them. The story is about being doers of the word, not just hearers. The foolish man heard the same words as the wise – he had the same knowledge – but he didn't apply what he'd heard. He didn't live it out. Therefore, his life was built on sand. Merely knowing, even believing, certain truths is not the whole of salvation. Seeking to live by these truths matters too.

That teaching by Jesus wasn't unusual. Immediately before the rock and sand illustration comes the forceful and frightening 'I never knew you' passage, a potential conversation between Jesus and people who expect entry into heaven but are turned away.

> Not everyone who says to me, 'Lord, Lord,' will enter the kingdom of heaven, but only he who does the will of my Father who is in heaven. Many will say to me on that day, 'Lord, Lord, did we not prophesy in your name, and in your name drive out demons and perform many miracles?' Then I will tell them plainly, 'I never knew you. Away from me, you evildoers!' (Matt. 7:21–3)

These people didn't do God's will. They reckoned they were Christians, and they claimed some spectacular Christian ministries. But maybe they warmed to the exciting, dramatic things of Christianity while missing fundamental issues of holiness. They certainly didn't do all God wanted. Therefore, though they claimed to know Jesus they were really strangers to him.

Similar principles are at stake behind Jesus's sheep-and-goats description of judgment. The 'sheep' had fed the hungry, given water to the thirsty, invited in strangers, clothed the naked, cared for the sick and visited the prisoners. The 'goats' had done none of these. The first were called blessed by the Father and welcomed to their inheritance in the kingdom. The second were cursed and doomed to eternal fire with the devil and his angels for company. The difference is not that one group knew Jesus and the other didn't – both refer to him as 'Lord' – but only one did what Jesus said.

Real faith shows. Real faith changes the way people live. The task of mission is not to bring about intellectual assent to a set of propositions about Jesus. It is to help people discover a faith which leads to obedience.

Hence the three-part agenda of the Great Commission: make disciples, baptise them, teach them to obey. The aim is that all three elements should be made complete in each individual. What comes into being is a new life of faith in Jesus, submission to Jesus and service for Jesus.

The goal of mission is to bring about individual salvation. People believe, and live out what they believe.

2. Doing God's works of love

When I was aged five, I ran across the road outside our home without looking for traffic, and was hit by a car which knocked me twenty-five feet down the road to land in a crumpled heap. My mother and a gaggle of neighbours picked me up, somehow got me inside the house, and nursed me better.

When I was aged seven, I tripped while trying to climb a barbed-wire fence, and ripped my leg open on the top strand of wire as I fell forward. Blood was everywhere. My father gathered me in his arms, carried me back over the fence, across a stream, over another fence, all the way across a huge field, over a gate, along a path and up the hill to our home. He collapsed in a chair while I was patched up by my mother.

When I was aged twelve, I was running fast over wet grass towards a gravel path. I slipped just where the edge of the grass joined the path and I fell. I could have saved myself by putting down my hand, but I was holding my new Instamatic camera and I wasn't going to let that get broken. So I held on tightly to it and allowed my knee to take the impact. Hundreds of tiny stones embedded themselves in the wound. My parents picked me up, carried me to the car, drove me home and helped me into a bath liberally laced with antiseptic.

Why did my parents bother? In any of these traumas, why not leave me lying in a blood-covered heap? Because they loved me. I was hurting, and they cared. Their actions had nothing to do with any merit in me. Far from it. I was endless hassle. Nor did their actions fit with their best time-management plans. In each case they had to give up what they were doing at that moment to meet my need. Nor could they anticipate any return on their investment in me. For all they knew I might turn into a rebellious teenager and leave home with hardly a glance over my shoulder. My parents helped me simply because they loved me. Love always cares.

That's why Jesus always cared for the needy people he met. For example, there was Bartimaeus. He was a man with little status, a blind beggar who depended on hand-outs to live. Jesus was passing nearby and Bartimaeus began to shout, 'Jesus, son of David have mercy on me!' (Mark 10:47) It would have been so easy for Jesus to ignore him. He was busy. There were huge crowds, lots of noise, countless requests. Why bother with one beggar? Bartimaeus kept shouting. Many told him to keep quiet, probably in strong terms. He didn't care, and went on calling, 'Son of David, have mercy on me!' Jesus stopped and had Bartimaeus come to him. He asked him what he wanted. 'Rabbi, I want to see' (Mark 10:51). The request was simple and full of faith. Jesus restored his sight and transformed Bartimaeus' life.

That wasn't a solitary act of mercy. Many times Jesus healed the sick. He delivered the demonised. He fed the hungry. He forgave sinners. He had no ulterior motives. He didn't do these things with conditions. He never said, 'I'll multiply these loaves and fishes so you have food providing afterwards you become my disciples.' Nor did he offer to heal the blind providing they became evangelists later. Nor did he forgive the sins only of those who pledged never to do those things again. Jesus's love carried no strings. Of course he longed for a response, but it would be a response made freely from gratitude for his goodness and from recognition of his lordship.

God loves people – all people – and Jesus brought that love down to earth. God's voice spoke through him; God's touch was felt through him; God's power was experienced through him; God's mercy was found through him. He made them well, he set them free, he fed their bodies, he gave them new lives. All that, simply because that's what love does when it encounters need.

John's gospel calls Jesus's miracles 'signs'. So they were. Of his power, yes, but of power shown in acts of love. Through Jesus God reached down from heaven and people sensed a touch of love.

The problem before the missionary in China, as I found it forty-five years ago, was not only how to save the souls of a fourth of the human race, but also how to save their bodies from perishing at the rate of four millions per annum, and to free their minds, more crippled than the feet of their women, from a philosophy and custom which had lasted for many centuries and left them at the mercy of any nation which might attack their country.

Timothy Richard, China missionary
Forty-five years in China: Reminiscences
(T. Fisher Unwin, 1916)

God hasn't lost his desire to touch people with his love. He cares that disease destroys lives, that millions are hungry, that so many are oppressed, that people live with guilt, fear and hopelessness. So he meets their need, and does so through the mouths, the hands, the feet he still has on earth. Our mouths, our hands, our feet as we embody his love.

> Over 1 billion people live in absolute poverty.
>
> Some 13 million under-fives die each year from malnutrition and related preventable diseases.
>
> Forty per cent of the population in sub-Saharan Africa is chronically malnourished.
>
> Seventy per cent of the planet's hungry are women and girls. Two out of every three illiterate people in the world are women.
>
> The UN estimate that 250 million children are being forced to work for their keep. At least five international networks exist for prostitution and trafficking of children.

I visited a small village on the edge of a town in South India. As we pulled up, I stepped out of the jeep on to a grass verge. 'Careful!' I was warned. 'Where you're standing is the only toilet area this village has.' I tiptoed my way off that verge, scattered the goats and pigs feeding there, and followed my guide into the tiny group of huts that formed the village. I've been around a bit, but seen little to match that poverty. The huts were made from mud and sticks, not fit to withstand any severe weather, offering little comfort against oppressive daytime heat or sharp cold at night. Under the rough blankets on which people lay was only earth. There were no roads nor proper paths. We scrambled between huts. In the door of one sat a wrinkled old woman. She was blind, devoid of any medical help or aids to ease her disability. At another was a boy, about six years old. His smile was unforgettable, but his face was a mass of sores. His father lifted up the lad's shirt to let me see his stomach and back covered in more sores. They had no money to get treatment. On we walked, meeting others as needy as these. It was a destitute place. No-one normally came there. No-one bothered with these people. No-one helped. For these were the lowest of the low, living on the edge of town because they were unacceptable in the larger community. The only income any of them had was from rag picking. Each day those who were fit went to the refuse tip, and scavenged for anything that could conceivably have some value. They filled large bags with it, brought it back to the village, sorted through it, and then tried to sell items in the market. Sometimes they'd have some reusable items of clothing. Often there was nothing other than polythene bags which they could persuade someone to buy. Many times their only income was a handful of rupees. These were the poorest of the poor.

No-one came to that village. No-one helped. Except some Christians. They visited, they helped, they taught. In the middle of the impoverished village was a small school. The teachers covered all the usual basic things children needed to know, and also taught the youngsters about Jesus. They gave time to these children so that they'd at least have the chance of a better life. Others wouldn't get involved. But God's servants did. It seemed like a shaft of God's love striking desperately needy people.

Then the King will say to those on his right, 'Come, you who are blessed by my Father; take your inheritance, the kingdom prepared for you since the creation of the world. For I was hungry and you gave me something to eat, I was thirsty and you gave me something to drink, I was a stranger and you invited me in, I needed clothes and you clothed me, I was sick and you looked after me, I was in prison and you came to visit me.'

Then the righteous will answer him, 'Lord, when did we see you hungry and feed you, or thirsty and give you something to drink? When did we see you a stranger and invite you in, or needing clothes and clothe you? When did we see you sick or in prison and go to visit you?'

The King will reply, 'I tell you the truth, whatever you did for one of the least of these brothers of mine, you did for me.'

Matt. 25:34–40

In one of India's big cities to the north I met a five-year-old boy. He'd been an orphan from very early in his life. When he was three, a couple adopted him. At last he had a family – acceptance, security, maybe even love. But almost as soon as the couple adopted the boy the woman discovered she was pregnant. Their own baby was born and as soon as they saw all was well, they got rid of the adopted lad. He was handed back as if he were an item from a store which could be returned as unsuitable or unnecessary. I met him where he lives now with other lads in a home run by Christians, people trying to give love to the unloved, trying to give hope to kids who would never otherwise have any hope. They were showing heaven's care on earth.

It's not different on the side of the world I'm more familiar with. I remember visiting a young priest living in one of the worst slums in Glasgow's Gorbals. All those old tenements are long since gone now, and they shouldn't have been there at the time I visited, for they were derelict, dirty and dangerous. The sanitation was minimal. The garbage was strewn everywhere. The rats were huge. The brickwork was crumbling. Roofs leaked, babies cried, people fought, drugs destroyed many, theft was common. It wasn't all bad. There were also saints there, and people looked out for each other more than happened in many a middle-class suburb. But to me it was a desperate and depressing place. No-one who'd grown up elsewhere chose to live there. Except that priest. He was an intelligent fellow, who probably could have been a success anywhere doing anything. But he was in the Gorbals because he wanted to live beside young people who faced a no-hope future, down-and-outs drinking themselves to death, single parents who struggled to provide for their children, and all the others who lived with emotional, relational or physical pain. That young priest's door was open to anyone, at any time. 'Don't you worry that your possessions will disappear out the door?' I asked, though he had precious little anyway. 'What I have is God's,' he said, 'and he'll always know where they are.' That reply could have been pious claptrap. From him it carried integrity. He was dying to self for Christ and for these people.

Care doesn't have to be that dramatic. I know a church which regularly feeds old people who otherwise wouldn't look after themselves properly and, in doing so, gives them a place to meet and find friendship. When the local community centre had no-one to run a youth club, some of the church members offered to take it on. Now there are dozens of kids who would be on the streets without it. A sheltered housing complex for the elderly was built nearby. Most of the residents aren't able to get out to church. So the local church came to them. Some members run a regular service there to which all are invited, and they visit the people in their own homes. That church also helps folk who are depressed, with people especially trained and qualified as counsellors. Students find homes away from home. The sick get prayed for as well as visited. Those who struggle with failure, even repeated sin, aren't condemned but accepted for the people of value they are. And on the list could run. It's not an exceptional church. There are many like that.

So there should be. The Father cares, therefore his children care. It's our mission to care. When others walk away we get involved. We interfere, for God's love doesn't allow us to turn our backs. The love of God mustn't just be talked about. It must be experienced. And it is, through medics who take their specialist skills to people who would otherwise get no healing; through agriculturalists trying to teach impoverished rural people to grow crops so they can feed their families; through engineers helping erect massive hydro-electric schemes to bring power to remote areas; through teachers who raise educational standards in countries which struggle to compete in an unequal world; through social workers who get alongside those who can't make it by themselves and who would be swept aside by others looking after their own interests. People take skills like these throughout the world.

They can be also used right where people are. Often no skill other than ordinary compassion is needed: visiting a lonely old person deserted by her family, helping the young mother overwrought by the incessant demands of her young children, taking time to listen to the over-stressed executive who's frightened of cracking, making friends with the family new to the area, going to see the colleague who's sick, staying late at work to help people meet deadlines, offering to drive someone to hospital, shopping for a disabled neighbour. And much more. This is for every Christian to do. It's not as if 'missionaries' should love and other

Christians needn't bother. Every child of God loves as his Father loves.

The calling – whatever kind, whatever location – is to share the gospel. Good news of a loving God will always be felt in works of mercy. Mission includes loving people in their need. That's legitimate and necessary.

I think I told you of our neighbour Wolo having died – the old man who had persisted time after time in burying living slaves with the corpses of his dead people. We have reason to fear that several lives were sacrificed at his funeral, but we have the satisfaction of knowing that we saved one poor woman. She had been bought a mile or two to the north of us, and as the buyers thought we might interfere if they brought her through our place, they decided to bring her down by canoe.

Just as they came opposite to our Station the woman began to shout, 'They are going to kill me! Come and take me, they are going to kill me!' Before they could gag her, our boys (school-boys and 'prentice lads) had caught the alarm, and divided into two parties. One took paddles and followed the canoe, and the other followed unseen along the path behind the trees on the river-bank. The people in the canoe (they were only two men besides the woman), finding themselves chased, pulled for the shore. But when they landed they found themselves between those who had followed close behind and those who had taken the path along the shore. Some of the townsmen, however, took their part, pointed their guns, and defied our boys to lay hands on the woman. Our youngsters, though they were quite unarmed, were strong in numbers (they were nearly forty) and in the courage of a good cause, and lifted the poor bound slave into the boat, and returned to our beach, not a little elated with their success.

George Grenfell, writing from Bolobo, Congo, 1894

3. Transforming or restoring fallen systems to God's pattern

Two friends of mine thought they'd found their dream cottage. The location was beautiful, nestling among gentle hills. The stonework was magnificent, the work of craftsmen. The decor was lovely, the size just right, the garden gorgeous. The dream lived until the nearby river overflowed and they found their cottage was right in its path. They learned it wasn't the first time it had happened, but the previous owner hadn't thought it helpful to tell them when he was selling the property. So the downstairs area of their home needed new carpets, new wall coverings and the replacement of many of their furnishings. Having done all that, what about the future? Did they move out before next winter came? Or did they hope that there wouldn't be so much rain next year? Or did they simply brace themselves for the next time they'd have to mop up the damage? None of those. With the help of the local council they got new drainage channels dug, routing the path of any flooding safely away from their cottage. For sure it would rain again next winter, and the river would overflow. They didn't just face that stoically and accept more destruction and hassle. They took action to change the consequences and make their home worth living in.

Likewise, if God's rule is ever to come on earth as it is in heaven, we can't merely keep on mopping up the damage done by sin and failure. We're not so helpless that we can do nothing other than spend our lives clearing up after the disasters of a fallen world. Mission includes searching out the causes of this world's failure and, as far as possible, putting them right. There are reasons why things happen as they do. If we can stop bad events repeating we should. That's bringing the world back under God's rule.

So, you don't just feed the hungry, you ask why they have no food. You don't just help the poor, you ask why financial institutions and governments keep people poor. You don't just help comfort victims of evil systems, you ask what can be done to change those systems. The answers you get give you an agenda for action.

The Old Testament prophets didn't merely wring their hands over the evils they saw. They denounced injustice and worked and campaigned to make change happen. So Nehemiah got Jerusalem's walls rebuilt. Haggai drove complacent people to prioritise the reconstruction of the Temple. Malachi strove to get the people to bring proper offerings. Virtually all of them stood against injustice, brought comfort to the oppressed, promised redemption for the righteous and pronounced condemnation for the guilty. They pointed out to people the way of God and urged them to go that way. 'He has showed you, O man, what is good. And what does the LORD require of you? To act justly and to love mercy and to walk humbly with your God' (Mic. 6:8).

Like Micah, Isaiah spoke words from God which made it clear that piety in a vacuum would not do. The people of his day prayed but also exploited their workers and quarrelled and fought with each other. They were two-faced. They would fast as if they were truly spiritual. But they took advantage of the weak and neglected the needy. God wasn't interested in their religious acts if there weren't also changed lives.

'Is not this the kind of fasting I have chosen:
to loose the chains of injustice
    and untie the cords of the yoke,
to set the oppressed free
    and break every yoke?
Is it not to share your food with the hungry
    and to provide the poor wanderer with shelter –
when you see the naked, to clothe him,
    and not to turn away from your own flesh and blood?
Then your light will break forth like the dawn,
    and your healing will quickly appear;
then your righteousness will go before you,
    and the glory of the LORD will be your rear guard.
Then you will call, and the LORD will answer;
    you will cry for help, and he will say: Here am I.'
(Isa. 58:6–9)

It took guts to speak out like that. These prophets weren't challenging the penniless and powerless but the wealthy and powerful, people with means to silence inconvenient voices. Many of the preachers paid a high price for their prophecies, but they had to deliver them. God's servants couldn't stay quiet and let evil reign unchallenged.

Jesus acted in the same tradition when he confronted the wrong-doing of his day. He overturned the tables of money-changers who abused the temple precincts. When legalists dragged an immoral woman before him and invited him to pronounce her death sentence, he challenged their attitudes and offered her mercy. He upset other social norms. He treated women with respect. He shared the company of tax-collectors. He allowed his disciples to pluck ears of corn on the Sabbath. He healed people on the Sabbath too. He touched lepers. He gave time to little children. He accepted a drink from a Samaritan woman. Jesus challenged many of the rules of his time. He disturbed vested interests, systems which gave people power and prestige. It's a major reason why they crucified him.

Mission has always involved challenging and transforming fallen systems, making those systems fit better with God's pattern.

In my office I have William Knibb's rocking chair. Its original owner was quite a man. He went as a Baptist missionary to Jamaica in 1825. He wasn't supposed to get involved in political issues, but Knibb could not ignore the desperate situation of slaves who were treated with shocking cruelty by plantation owners. He sided with them, much to the annoyance of the owners. When the slaves rebelled in late 1831 Knibb and other missionaries were jailed, though almost certainly they had no part in the insurrection. After a few months Knibb was released and sailed back to Britain. Once home he and other missionaries began a campaign to get slavery abolished in the British Empire. Up and down the country they toured, stirring people to action. They gave evidence before Committees of the House of Commons and the House of Lords. Eventually an Act went through Parliament in 1833 which abolished slavery from the following year. Knibb's name is not the best known in the anti-slavery campaign. But when he returned to Jamaica he and his fellow missionaries were heroes. At great risk and with tireless energy they had fought for the powerless and won their freedom.

Mission must always oppose evil and try to change it. Exploitation and abuse happen in politics, economics, commerce, law, ecology and countless other spheres of life. Christians can't run from these, holding up their hands in horror and promising never to get involved. There's always something we can do, even if only a little. A candle may not give much light, but blow it out and all you're left with is darkness.

> Throughout the world one person is killed or maimed every 20 minutes by mines. There are an estimated 110 million unexploded mines strewn over 64 countries. Between 5 and 10 million more are produced each year. For every mine cleared, 20 are laid. More have died from landmines than from either poisonous gases or nuclear weapons.

There's much that Christians should be angry about in today's world. Young men and women forced to walk through minefields in front of soldiers so that they are maimed and killed rather than the troops. Anti-personnel landmines scattered across countries, killing more civilians after a war than the total number of casualties during the war. Nations crippled with immense debts forced to take loans or aid with strings which will sentence them to deeper debt and greater poverty from which they can never be free. Children used as sex slaves. Five-, six-, seven-year-olds chained to looms – sold to a factory owner to offset a family debt – working 12 to 15 hours a day. Elderly people abandoned by families. Drug companies, finding they can't get licences in the West for medicines not considered sufficiently safe, offloading them in the developing world. Baby-milk manufacturers persuading mothers in the developing world not to breastfeed but use powdered milk instead, resulting in the deaths of many babies from inadequate nutrition and poor hygiene. Governments approving crude methods of torture against their political prisoners. A cynical disregard by governments or powerful industries for pollution which is killing whole communities. On and on and on the list could run.

Christians get frightened that they become agitators, sidelined from their real task of proclaiming the message of individual salvation. Or they're scared that they set themselves up as God, approving some actions and disapproving of others. But while we've questioned our motives or methods evil has triumphed, people have suffered, and God's rule over this world has been diminished.

The temptation has been to write off this world and live merely for the next. God hasn't done that, for there are still people he loves who are hurting and need help. As God's children – as his agents of love – we can't stand by watching evil triumph. We speak for the voiceless. We act for the powerless. We do so for a God who wants his people rescued and his kingdom to come for all. 'For the creation was subjected to frustration, not by its own choice, but by the will of the one who subjected it, in hope that the creation itself will be liberated from its bondage to decay and brought into the glorious freedom of the children of God' (Rom. 8:20–1). That liberation is the ultimate goal. It's a hope which isn't going to be fulfilled completely until Jesus returns and the world as we know it ends. But it doesn't all have to wait until then. It's on God's agenda now: good news for the poor, freedom for the prisoners, sight for the blind, release for the oppressed. 'Your kingdom come, your will be done on earth as it is in heaven.' We can't pray for it without working for it.

This is mission on a big scale. It aims to change individuals. It shows God's love wherever there's need. It takes on the worst of the world's evils and tries to restore God's rule. It's radical mission. We are in the business of changing the world.

I picture a house in a state of disrepair. The roof leaks, windows are broken, wallpaper is peeling, the garden is overgrown, there's rot in the timbers, the place is untidy. The problem is not that the house was badly built, but it's been poorly maintained by lazy, careless occupants. But the day comes when something changes deep inside those tenants. They begin to care. How they live, and the place in which they live, starts to matter to them. The roof and windows get mended, new wallpaper decorates the rooms, weeds are evicted from the back plot, rot is treated, furniture is put in order. The place doesn't become perfect for these people aren't perfect. But at last it resembles the home it was meant to be. At last it's a place that once again brings honour to its architect, builder and owner.

I believe in mission that aims for this world again to be a place that brings honour to its architect, builder and owner.

Chapter 6

Getting called

I KNEW GOD was calling me. I was eighteen, and I'd been a Christian for a whole six weeks. Baptised that morning, I was back for the evening service brimming with commitment. The sermon that night was about Stephen. Here was a man, the preacher stressed, who literally gave his whole life for Christ. Didn't God want our whole lives too? What was that going to mean in practice? I felt challenged.

In one sense I knew God already had my whole life. I was willing to do anything and go anywhere. Until then I'd assumed my future would be in journalism. I wanted to be a Christian reporter, to write well, to write honestly, and use the power of the pen for good in the world.

But from that sermon on I wasn't at peace with that. Others could be journalists. God wanted something more from me. I felt called. But to what? If God had some special plan for my life, what was it? I didn't know but I was determined to find out.

I prayed. How I prayed! Day and night I prayed. Over and over I told God I wanted to know his will. Even if it was months or years, I'd keep praying. On and on, whatever it took. No sacrifice too great. No time too long. No mystery too deep. I'd find God's plan. After five days of thinking like that, I reckoned there had to be an easier way.

'Okay,' I said, 'God must surely want me where there's greatest need in the world. So where's that?' By the next evening I had the answer: missionary work overseas. It was an answer deeply embedded in my heart ever since I saw lantern slides at a church meeting when I was three. Besides, God confirmed it the very next day because my eye had caught a newspaper headline about suffering in Third World countries. A sign. Nothing could be clearer.

It wouldn't be easy though. My teen years had been laced with stories of martyrdom in the Congo rebellion and I knew that a missionary career could be terminal. Only one thing would be worse. Suppose I disappeared into the depths of the jungle and never got married? 'But' – no sooner had the problem arisen than it had been resolved – 'nothing is too hard for God.' He knew my need and he'd supply it. So, I'd be a missionary and he'd provide a wife with beauty, charm, godliness, passion for the lost, and who was tough enough to eat crocodiles for breakfast.

I told my minister about my call. He looked happy enough, though he must have reckoned this rush of enthusiasm couldn't entirely be trusted to last. 'I'll put obstacles in your way,' he said, 'because your call needs to be tested. If it's really from God it won't go away.' I beamed at him confidently. He could ask me to wrestle with lions and I'd endure. Nothing was too difficult.

Except telling my parents. I dreaded it. They'd been so pleased that I was the first in the family line ever to move into anything remotely like a prosperous, high-flying career, off to the big city for fame and fortune. They'd be disappointed I was giving it up. For days I worried, then got friends to pray for me while I made a special journey home. The words came stumbling out, 'I'm going to be a missionary.' My mother smiled with quiet pride, then hugged me. My father said, 'Fine, but why did you come home specially?'

Days became weeks, and weeks became months. I met with the local representative of a missionary society, talked with others about what I might do, and began night school to acquire more qualifications to get on the course of theological study I knew would come later. All seemed well.

Except deep inside I was beginning not to be so sure. I knew God had called me to something special, but was it really to be a missionary? Sure, there was a need, but was the need the call? My inner peace was being disturbed.

One night I knelt to pray. I never knelt usually, but this was special. 'God, just what do you want?' I stayed quiet, and waited. Seconds later two words flashed through my head: 'The ministry.'

It felt like God had spoken. I got off my knees, thanked God for his help, and went to bed.

I was grateful but not excited. Being a minister didn't thrill me. Thinking up two new sermons each week seemed impossible, terrifying and boring. Where was the romance of going to some far-off country, converting the heathen, and then returning to show my slides and tell amazing stories? But if it was what God wanted . . .

So began years of study and years of ministry. It's always been hard but never boring. I've plumbed depths that felt unbearable, wondering if there was any future worth living for. I've soared to heights of joy, feeling I was getting an advance taste of heaven. Through the length, breadth, height and depth of it all, I've known this was God's will for me. Along with just a few other things, that's one of the certainties of my life. That was what God called me to.

Then, unexpectedly, God brought me full circle to where I am now, leading a mission agency which is trying to make Jesus known in countries all round the world. It's the very same society of which I had made enquiries twenty-seven years previously, which must rank as one of the longest job applications on record. Every day I'm working directly to get the gospel out to people who've never heard. Maybe the first sense of call wasn't a hundred per cent wrong.

That's my story – the short version! It's not neat and tidy. I wish God sent personal letters detailing his plan for our lives. I wish being in the will of God meant all the minutiae fell neatly into place. Rarely, virtually never, is it like that. Almost always calls are messy things.

The rest of this chapter explores some general but sensitive issues about being called to mission. The next chapter homes in on the specific issue of working out if we have a special calling to mission work.

Who's called?

'At this convention,' the speaker said with solemn excitement, 'many now serving on the mission field first heard their call. They came here thinking it was just another Christian meeting. Now they're in India, Nigeria, Brazil, Papua New Guinea, or any of a hundred other countries. They didn't expect to hear God call them. But he did. Tonight it may be you. Tonight may change your life.'

I heard the speaker begin his talk like that at a major Christian conference. The logic behind the preacher's words was fairly simple:

- Most Christians spend their lives on ordinary things, family, home, career, local church.
- Some Christians are selected by God to be missionaries. They're special people, different from the rest, and they go far away to tell people about Jesus.

The speaker must have thought he was inspiring his audience by stressing they were in God's firing line. He was wrong. Since most people don't want to go far away from family, career and comfort, most had absented themselves from that meeting or were keeping their profile low to make sure God didn't spot them in the crowd. They didn't want to find themselves in the repertoire of next year's conference speaker.

But the fundamental premise of that preacher was wrong. God doesn't call some to mission but not most. He doesn't pick a few and make them responsible for winning the world, while the rest get on with ordinary things like careers and bringing up children. He doesn't make the Great Commission the responsibility of a spiritual elite and leave the plebs to do background tasks like attending missionary prayer meetings or hosting missionary teas. There aren't two groups. Mission is everyone's calling.

For example, two of the most successful evangelists in the early days of the Church were Stephen and Philip. Both appear in the list of those appointed to distribute food fairly to widows. Neither said, 'I'm a waiter: that's my role. Don't expect me to share my faith as well.' Stephen got into serious debates about the faith, and was very effective. So powerful was his witness that they got rid of him, and he became the first Christian martyr. Philip was among those who left Jerusalem when major persecution began. He went to Samaria, told people there about Jesus, and there was a mass turning to Christ. Later he deliberately began to evangelise an Ethiopian in his chariot, and that man came to faith.

These people were simply getting on with ordinary Christian lives. There was no dramatic or special 'call', no being sent off deliberately to far-away places, no exceptional talent or gifting for communicating the faith. Witness is what they did wherever they were, for it was the general calling of every Christian. The Holy Spirit was sent to all Christians precisely so that all Christians could tell others about Jesus. The power they received enabled them to witness everywhere, even to the ends of the earth. But that anointing was also so the gospel could be told in Jerusalem. The gospel was for relatives, for next-door neighbours, for people in the local market. The Holy Spirit wasn't given only to those heading out of Jerusalem to spread the gospel to the rest of the world.

> But you will receive power when the Holy Spirit comes on you; and you will be my witnesses in Jerusalem, and in all Judea and Samaria, and to the ends of the earth.
>
> Acts 1:8

It is fundamental that every Christian is a witness for Jesus. The Great Commission is for all disciples. A missionary God only has missionary children.

However, in biblical times there were also those who were chosen for particular work, something which would take them beyond the ordinary and everyday. The classic example is the call of Barnabas and Saul to go on missionary journeys. They were an established part of the leadership team at Antioch. But God had a bigger plan for their lives:

In the church at Antioch there were prophets and teachers: Barnabas, Simeon called Niger, Lucius of Cyrene, Manaen (who had been brought up with Herod the tetrarch) and Saul. While they were worshipping the Lord and fasting, the Holy Spirit said, 'Set apart for me Barnabas and Saul for the work to which I have called them.' So after they had fasted and prayed, they placed their hands on them and sent them off. (Acts 13:1–3)

This is special. These were not men asked to witness and work for Christ simply where they were, continuing to do what they always did. They left Antioch, sailed first to Cyprus, and then on to many other places in their known world. They were the first travelling evangelists of the Christian Church.

That was the ministry for which they had been specially called by God. The work was his choice, and so were they as the people to do that work. God decided, somehow revealed their names to the Church, and they were 'sent on their way by the Holy Spirit' (Acts 13:4). This was God's initiative. So it continued. God moved them from place to place, bringing many to faith through their witness.

Therefore there is one calling but sometimes a specialised role for that calling to be fulfilled.* There is the general calling to witness for every Christian. It's the instinct in the heart of all who are children of God, the command of Christ to all who are his disciples, the work of all who are given the Holy Spirit. No-one is missed or excused. All are called to mission in that general sense. There is also a specific role of mission work for some. God chooses people for particular tasks in particular places at particular times. Why he calls some and not others is often a mystery. Paul, for example, thought it amazing that God should choose him, a person who had persecuted the Church. But God did, and still takes people who would never be short-listed by ordinary criteria. No-one can ever say, 'God wouldn't call me,' or, 'God couldn't use me.' He's called and used some very strange people in the past, so why would any of us be excused?

*Most people speak about those who are 'called to mission work'. Often they get referred to as missionaries. Though I use terminology like that all of the time it's misleading, as if some aren't missionaries and are not called to mission work. But I admit it's unacceptably clumsy to refer to 'those with a specialised role for their general call to mission to be fulfilled'. So, to a large extent, I'll conform to convention and talk of those called specially to do mission. But it's always with the qualification that all are called and only the specific role or context varies.

Problems

Often this business of being called goes wrong in either of two ways. One is when people don't realise they have a general calling to mission but do. The other is when people think they have a specific calling to mission but don't.

The second of these is a large part of what the next chapter tries to resolve. The first should never be an issue, largely for the reason in Chapter 1, that mission is in the heart of God and will be in the heart of all his children. In recent times, though, two things have caused problems with accepting the general call to mission.

One arises because we're led by our feelings more than almost any generation before us. It's our luxury. Go back a generation or two and people didn't expect to feel comfortable, sometimes not even to enjoy life. They didn't have the money to indulge, they might not have the health to be active, and tomorrow was a very uncertain day. If they made decisions based on their feelings, they didn't make great choices. The hard truth was that life was tough and that couldn't be changed. People had to grit their teeth and get on with what needed to be done. Not now. Now we think it unfair if life doesn't feel good, if we're not happy, if circumstances and events aren't working to our advantage. If something makes us uncomfortable we don't join in. If anything threatens our well-being we avoid it. We do what we *like* and don't do what we *dislike*. There's a lot less teeth gritting than there used to be.

The other point is semi-theological. These last years have seen an explosion in teaching on the gifts of the Spirit. It's been strongest in Pentecostal and charismatic churches, but not just there. Almost everyone has been told, 'God has given you gifts. Discover which are yours, and use them. And don't covet gifts you haven't got.' Many don't feel gifted for witnessing. One specific passage seems to confirm that:

> It was he who gave some to be apostles, some to be prophets, some to be evangelists, and some to be pastors and teachers.
>
> Eph. 4:11

In Ephesians 4 there's a strong stress on different ministries with which God has gifted the Church. People know that not everyone is an apostle, or a prophet, or a pastor/teacher. Logically they reason that they're not all evangelists. Since no-one finds evangelism easy and painless, and next to no-one has instant success at helping people find faith, most conclude God hasn't gifted them as evangelists. Since they're not gifted, it's not their calling and not their responsibility. So they'll leave witness to those God has called.

Both of those problems should not exist. Each has flawed biblical logic. The first is flawed by elevating feelings until they're virtually a god. Our pleasure, comfort, or self-interest shouldn't control what we do. That's how non-Christians live. Christians follow Jesus. He owned less than foxes because he had nowhere of his own to lay his head. He set aside his own will in order to do whatever God wanted. He accepted pain and death in order that we would escape penalty and live. He promised nothing less, nothing better than his experience to those who followed him. Mission hurts. People die sharing their faith. But there's no alternative. As someone has said, you can't take off your faith like a jacket on a hot day. You can't drop one part of being a disciple and keep the rest. There's no opt-out from suffering for God and the gospel that leaves us inside Christianity.

Brother will betray brother to death, and a father his child; children will rebel against their parents and have them put to death. All men will hate you because of me . . .

A student is not above his teacher, nor a servant above his master. It is enough for the student to be like his teacher, and the servant like his master. If the head of the house has been called Beelzebub, how much more the members of his household!

Matt. 10:21–2, 24–5

The flaw in the mistaken idea that only the gifted should witness is the failure to understand a simple principle that what may be special responsibilities for some are often still general responsibilities for everyone. For example, I'm not a lifeguard – not trained as one, not employed as one, not dressed as one – but if

I was walking by a river and saw a child in the water struggling for life I'd plunge in and save him. Saving drowning people is not my special role in life, but if someone needs to be rescued of course I'll try to do it. There are lots of examples like that. It's not much different with mission. Telling others of Jesus is a general calling, something arising from a common passion to let the lost know of a loving God. Some have a special calling for a special role in mission, a calling to get training, give time, go places, take on extraordinary tasks. The specialness of mission for some doesn't remove it from everyone else. God's Church requires both. It needs the whole vast army of people witnessing to their faith. It also needs commandos and marines who do particular work.

- I'm no horticulturist but I dig my garden . . .
- I'm no ornithologist but I feed birds . . .
- I'm no electrician but I change light bulbs . . .
- I'm no taxi-driver but I take my daughter to school . . .

- Who'd say 'I'm no cook' and starve to death for lack of making a meal?
- Who'd say 'I'm no laundryman' and have people stay clear of them for want of washing their clothes?
- Who'd say 'I'm no fireman' and watch an overheated pan set the house on fire?
- Who'd say 'I'm no doctor' and do nothing for their child who's fallen and hurt himself?

No-one escapes the general call to mission. No-one can say, 'Witness is not for me.' The critical question is not whether we're called, for we are. The critical question is 'Where am I called to?' The answer may be to serve Jesus right where we are already, among those we live with and work beside. That is a wholly legitimate calling. Or the answer may be to work for Jesus in a new place, perhaps among people with different backgrounds to our own. That special call to mission is real too. Both are valid.

Looking for volunteers?

Joe's an enthusiast. Reads his Bible, says his prayers, attends church meetings, talks to others about Jesus. He turns up on his minister's doorstep one day, saying he feels he should be a missionary. Minister is overjoyed. Church is overjoyed. They've never had one of their members become a missionary before. At last someone has offered to go. They recommend him warmly to a mission agency. The agency is impressed with Joe and the church's backing of Joe, and within a year he's off to win the world.

Is that how the world's missionary force should be formed? It's often how it is. It has all sorts of dangers, not the least of which is that the church may be so enamoured of the idea of Joe becoming a missionary, or so impressed with his sense of calling, that they don't choose to tell the mission agency that Joe has started ten different projects in the last two years and never finished any of them. Nor do they mention that Joe is a smooth-talking charmer who has played havoc with the emotions of every young lady in the church, and that his sensitivity to people's feelings scores about minus 5 on a scale of 1 to 10. If they knew these things most mission agencies would instantly be hesitant. But, because Joe is so good with words and so confident of his calling, and because he comes with impeccable references from his church, they enrol him gladly and only find out the problems later. Those problems will come out, and usually worse than before. Place someone out of his own culture, alongside colleagues with whom he may have no natural affinity, and give him work to do which is stressful and often unfruitful, and personality flaws increase rather than reduce. Joe may well have a miserable time as a missionary, and cause big problems for others too.

That's not an unusual scenario. And it'll keep happening as long as everything hinges on volunteers. We wait for a divine blob of calling to drop from heaven, after which those on whom it has fallen offer their services to churches and mission agencies, and then they become the superhuman characters called missionaries.

It doesn't have to be like that. Maybe it shouldn't be.

Peter and John went from Jerusalem to Samaria following Philip's preaching there. Philip had done a good job but there was unfinished work of discipleship, so the apostles went to do it. It's perhaps the first example in the New Testament of anyone deliberately crossing a cultural boundary to do Christian work. (Philip seems to have fled to Samaria. It was a useful move, but not by choice.) Were Peter and John volunteers? Acts 8:14 says they were 'sent' by the other apostles. The Greek word used there is from the verb *apostellō*. It has the sense of commissioning. Peter and John were people under orders. They didn't go because it was their idea or their wish.

Virtually the same word with the same meaning occurs in Acts 11:22 when the Jerusalem church sent Barnabas to look after the new-born church at Antioch. The Greek word is *exapostellō*. (The prefix *ex* adds the sense of 'away' or 'out', so the emphasis is on sending Barnabas away from Jerusalem to Antioch.) The church decided Barnabas should take on this work.

Barnabas soon realised he needed help. He went to Tarsus, found Paul, and Acts 11:26 says he 'brought' him to Antioch. This time the Greek word is *agō*. It might be used simply meaning 'to lead away'. But it often implied force. It was the word used for someone driving off another person's cattle, or for bringing someone to court for justice. I wonder how much choice Paul had about going with Barnabas!

Similarly I wonder how much choice the two of them had when they were chosen by the Spirit to leave Antioch and begin their wider missionary work. They were set apart and sent off, with not a hint that they had any right to refuse. This was the Spirit's decision, accepted and confirmed by the local church. So they went.

What is significant in these examples is where the initiative lies. The apostles saw a need in Samaria, so they sent Peter and John. The Jerusalem church saw a need in Antioch, so they sent Barnabas. Barnabas found a greater need than he could meet in Antioch, so he fetched Paul. The Antioch church were told to release their two leading members for work elsewhere, so they commissioned Barnabas and Paul. Not once is the initiative with the person who goes. Always it is with God or with God's people. There are no interviews by elders or deacons. There are no applications to mission agencies. There are not even prayer times or candidate boards to decide whether or not someone who thinks he's called really is called. There are none of these because there are no volunteers. No-one offers service. The decision for someone to go is the Church's, not the missionary's.

We call the Church the army of God, but we're not much like an army and certainly not in this matter of choosing who to send for the hardest and most important work. Armies don't issue instructions like 'The battle begins tomorrow at nine. Those volunteering to fight should show up ten minutes before then with rifles at the ready. Those not wishing to fight are advised to stay in their billets lest any stray bullets come their way.' How many battles would be won? Or suppose a commander couldn't choose the right men and women in his battalion for the most dangerous tasks, because the toughest and most talented had chosen to do the administration, or cook the meals, or drive the trucks, or issue the camp newsletter, or organise the battalion football team. All he was allowed to do was appeal for volunteers and then do his best with those who offered. How could he defeat the enemy if most of his crack troops had the right to opt out of fighting? How can the Church do mission effectively when leaders can't assign people to roles that are right for them and needed to advance the kingdom? How can the Church have a cutting edge when a leader can only appeal for volunteers and make the best of whoever shows up, no matter how they're gifted? How can there be co-ordination and harmony when everyone self-selects their role? How can leaders avoid being dogged with frustration and failure when usually the suitable aren't available and the available aren't suitable?

The remarkable thing is that the volunteer system behind most mission work has produced some highly effective people. Heroes and heroines abound. They have done great things. They sensed God's call and responded. But how many sensed God's call and didn't respond? How much more might have been done if Christian leaders had been able to send those with the right skills and right experience to do critical work for the kingdom? How much better would it be if church leaders were able to scan their congregations and call people into areas of work for which they're ideally suited?

Of course all that smacks of authoritarianism. And those who have abused leadership with crude and unbiblical attempts to run people's lives have much to answer for. There has been serious damage when domineering leaders have manipulated people to serve their own ends. The rest of us, trying to honour individual rights and responsibility, have reacted by steering well clear of anything that has even a hint of running other people's lives. But abuses shouldn't spoil the genuine work of leadership. The Bible doesn't hesitate to use words like 'obey' and 'submit', and though caution is wise we must not be so nervous of leadership that we fail to recognise the directive voice of God through those he sets over us.

> Obey your leaders and submit to their authority. They keep watch over you as men who must give an account. Obey them so that their work will be a joy, not a burden, for that would be of no advantage to you.
>
> Heb. 13:17

I've been helped that way. Despite my initial guidance, for a time I lost confidence in my sense of call into full-time Christian work. For a year I took an office job. To my own surprise I enjoyed it and did quite well. I soared upwards from the lowly role of office assistant to the dizzy heights of senior office assistant! I could have had a long-term career in administration. But I'd gone to help a small church, and the leader, Harry, asked me to preach. I wasn't sure I wanted to, but he insisted. I gave it my best. Afterwards Harry drew me aside and said, 'Perhaps there's a gift going to waste in an office.' That was all. It was enough, along with a newly stirring inner conviction, to get me back on track.

Not for a moment do I mean anyone should be forced into Christian service without their own sense of call. I doubt anyone could last without believing to the core of their being that what they do is God's will. You're exhausted physically, emotionally and spiritually, knowing that you're only going to get a few hours' sleep before you get up and do it all again tomorrow; you've faced poverty, abuse, addiction, death, birth, suffering, loneliness, and that's just this week; you've worked twice as long and twice as hard as most others but yet they criticise what you've done; you've given up a high income and comfortable lifestyle, asked your family to share many sacrifices, and there's not a lot of evidence that the world's been changed. When that's how it is – and it's often like that – you don't keep going unless you believe your work is what God wants of your life. Without a deep conviction of God's call you'd soon opt for a quieter and easier life.

But not everything about a call should rest with the individual. Individuals don't have to be the first to recognise God's choice, nor the first to do something about it, nor the sole judge of whether that call is valid. Church leaders who hold to the lofty principle that they must never be directive to people about their Christian work or priorities with their time may be quenching one of God's ways of speaking to those he has made them responsible for. Where would David have been without the intervention of Samuel? He might have spent his life tending sheep.

There must be more to appointing people to key mission positions than waiting to see who volunteers. God doesn't speak only to individuals. He also tells churches to set people apart for him, and church leaders must have the courage to take the initiative. It's scary to intervene in case you get it wrong. And giving guidance to another person seems presumptuous. But both of those can be excuses for failing to take risks, or, to put that more spiritually, for failing to live by faith.

Validating a call

Where there's a vital need for all-round honesty and involvement is when a potential mission worker is past the first stage and a decision has to be made whether or not a sense of call is for real. Too often there's been an unwillingness to disappoint eager volunteers. They're so sincere; they're making sacrifices; they're the first missionaries from that church in living memory. But sometimes every church member knows they don't get on easily with others, they often don't keep their promises, they've never got involved in evangelism work in the church, and they hold some very strange views. Well, let's recommend them anyway. Presumably the mission agency knows the kind of people it wants, and perhaps everything will be different when they're on the mission field.

But mission agencies can't know those they interview the way their local church knows them. No amount of mission expertise compares in value with years of observing someone's Christian life and work. And rarely is anything different in the sense of better on the mission field. The stresses are greater, the work harder and the support sometimes less. Weaknesses are magnified, not diminished.

No-one wants to hurt someone's feelings, especially when the issue of whether or not to be a missionary has been mulled over and prayed about for a long time, and often the plan is well known to everyone including the present employer. It's especially difficult for friends in a local church to be negative. But a call isn't valid unless shared – like one person's guidance before marriage isn't to be accepted unless the intended partner gets the same guidance. In the case of mission there are lots of partners whose leading must all be the same. As well as the potential missionary, usually that's also his or her church, a mission agency, and a local church or union of churches in another country. All must believe the same. If they do, that harmony of thought is persuasive evidence of God's will. Without it plans must be rethought.

Everyone is responsible for the outcome. No-one can leave the choice to others. No-one can afford to hope someone else will do the dirty work of saying 'no' to a person who's going down the wrong road.

That needs courage and honesty. But it's vital. No-one is helped when uncritical recommendations are made. The missionary suffers; colleagues suffer; locals suffer; the mission agency suffers; the sending church suffers. Usually the best judge of suitability is the local church. Churches have a responsibility to send those God has called. They have an equal responsibility not to send those God hasn't called.

In the general sense, everyone is called to mission. No-one misses that call. God has given his Spirit to every Christian because every Christian is a witness. Some are called to do particular work in the world. How they get called to that is sometimes quietly, sometimes dramatically. Everything will fall neatly into place, so people think. It doesn't. There can be many problems, many struggles, and much pain. But there's no opt-out clause in case of difficulty. God's call is non-negotiable.

When I first sensed a special call to service for God I wrote to the principal of a theological college, asking what I would need to do if I was to train for Christian work. When I read his reply, I almost wished I'd never asked. He listed course after course he thought I should take. My heart sank. I didn't want to do all that. All I was after was a quick route into service for God. Then I read the last line of his letter: 'The work and the master are worthy of the best.' That sentence ingrained itself in my mind. In the end I did far more than the principal ever suggested. I don't regret it. When God calls us to serve him, his work and his lordship of our lives are worthy of the very best.

The next chapter is about trying to be sure that God really is calling us. If we're going to sign away our careers and perhaps take our families to the ends of the earth, we'd better get our guidance right.

Chapter 7

Working out the call

GOD'S VOICE WOULDN'T be picked up on a tape recorder, but he speaks. He calls people to mission. That's everyone generally, and it's some people especially for particular types of mission work.

How do we know if we're in that second group? I've spent a lot of time with people who are asking that question, and I know how much of a struggle it is to be sure enough to make decisions. The bigger the changes that will follow, the more certain people need to be. It can mean uprooting a whole family, leaving other relatives and friends, trying to adjust to a very different culture, learning a new language, facing new work, taking new risks. It means abandoning the security base we've known all our lives, the significance of which hits us only when we face losing it. Almost everything may be turned upside down. No-one should do that on a whim. No-one dare do it without a high level of confidence that it's God's will. So this chapter is for those at that point in life. If that's not where you are, you should still read it in case you should be! Maybe God's speaking and you're not listening.

Is the need the call?
So many didn't know of Jesus. So many were suffering hunger, oppression, sickness, deprivation. I had a choice: stay with the pleasant lifestyle to which I was becoming accustomed, or give my life for those who had so little. It didn't seem to take a lot of prayer to know which was right. The need was the call.

So I thought at the time. Many do. It's simple logic. It can't be right to ignore the plight of those worse off than I. Their need is my call. But it isn't, or at least not in that simplistic sense.

First, it's not the call because not everyone can meet every need no matter how great it is. There's a great need to feed the hungry in Africa. Millions are malnourished, and many die because of conditions related to that. But suppose every Christian in the world rushed to Africa to deal with the problem. There would be instant overcrowding in some African nations, and sudden and serious deprivation in countries those Christians had left. It would be like a liner which had been overbalancing to port suddenly keeling to starboard because every passenger rushed across the deck to cure the list to port. Put in crude terms like this, the need cannot be the call for everyone.

Second, it's not the call because need alone doesn't determine who's right or best to meet the need. I might be overwhelmed by stories of poor residents in a remote area dying of appendicitis. They would have been cured if only there had been a doctor there to operate. So I dash off to that remote area to meet the need. Are they helped? Only to an even earlier grave. For I'm no medical doctor, and if I started opening them up with a scalpel I'd kill them. I could have the best intentions in the world but I don't have the skill to make them well. My awareness of their need does not constitute a call for me to be the one to help them.

Third, the need isn't the call because there are more choices than meeting the need or doing nothing about it. It had seemed to me I could either opt for a selfish, comfortable life, or I could leave it all to help others. Put like that, the choice was obvious. But those weren't the only options. I didn't have to keep all my money for myself; I could direct it to help mission happen in the world through others. My career didn't have to be for self-advancement; I could be a journalist who used his skills to benefit others. There were many other things I could do: pray, enthuse, inform, stir, campaign, change my own lifestyle, do mission close to home. It was never a stark 'Go and meet the need or do nothing'. In the end I sensed God calling me into church-based ministry, but I also felt him say that if I did he would use me to bring others to serve in mission throughout the world. That has happened, and is hap-pening today.

It's too crude to say the need is the call. An army commander places his troops in many strategic positions, not just at the point where the attack will come. He has a big plan in mind, one designed to win the whole war and not just to meet the demands of one battle. Likewise God puts his children in many places, each with different roles. He can't have everyone rush to just one trouble-spot, for that would leave other vital tasks undone and vital areas unmanned.

Is the need never the call? We can't say that, for sometimes it is. If a child rushes out of my neighbour's house covered in flames, that child's need is most certainly my call to whip off my coat and smother the flames. If I don't, he'll die. I can't argue, 'This is not my child. He's not really my responsibility. Someone else should be putting out these flames.' At that moment those issues are irrelevant. It would be terrible to do nothing. The child has an immense need, and I'm the only one there who can meet it, so his need is my call.

There are dramatic and less dramatic parallels to that in Christian work. A situation arises when a witness needs to be given, an act of kindness done, a stand taken, and we're the ones on the spot at that moment. It's not a time to say, 'The need isn't the call.' Or, in a more general sense, we can be uniquely placed to meet a need. We have the money, the time, the ability, the experience, or the relationship to make something happen. My friend Andrew had the electrical skills and the time to rewire a hospital in an impoverished area in Central America. He heard of the need, knew he could meet it and, with help from others, went and got the job done. Wasn't that a call from God? It was, but the call emerged out of an awareness of need. Sometimes it's like that. Need should always make us ask, 'Does God want me to do something about this?'

We can't meet every need. Every need isn't our call, and we shouldn't jump from emergency to emergency as if it was. But that doesn't mean we're deaf and blind to the unexpected crises around us. Jesus was proactive and reactive in his ministry. He never sacrificed his long-term sense of purpose but he responded to urgent needs as they arose. Our calling to mission will, ideally, be not far different from that.

What, though, of the more general issue of being called to some form of mission work? Lots of people have some sense of that, maybe quite vague: 'I just know there's something God wants me to do.' It's a feeling of being set apart for special work, even though there's no particular need to meet or job to do. How can we be sure when God is speaking? How do we know we're not just imagining it?

Knowing you're called

If only God would write his will in the sky... I've often wished that. Knowing what God wants isn't easy. Knowing you're called to a special mission task has some similarity to knowing whether you've met the right person to marry. For both you need enough confidence to commit your whole life. For neither does it feel like you're that sure.

In this section I'm going to write about what it feels like to be called. But I need to give three warnings. First, it's describing the indescribable. You can't put the call of God in a test-tube and measure its component parts. It's spiritual, and our limited vocabulary and limited understanding will never fully comprehend it. Second, it's different for everyone. God doesn't follow a formula. He met with Moses at a burning bush. He called Isaiah during a vision. Paul saw a blinding light. There's no foolproof pattern so when it happens you know for sure it's God you're dealing with. Third, no-one can ever have proof. No matter how many signs, voices, coincidences or anything else, everything is open to interpretation. Nothing will remove all mystery.

Those qualifications in place, let's move through a number of ways by which people feel called by God. Just one final, final qualification as we start on that. The instinct is to tick off the different points that follow, feeling ever more called if you get several. So, for example, scoring a hit with one form of guidance equals being stirred by God. Scoring a hit with two or three means God unquestionably wants you as a missionary. Scoring with more than four means you're the apostle Paul's replacement. No, it doesn't. Guidance can't be ticked off like that. There are some who have served God magnificently in mission work who could never discern any specific moment or sign of being called. For your spiritual health neither overrate nor underrate what follows.

Gut feeling

This ranks at number one. People know they're called because they know they're called. Profound, that.

Of course gut feelings are utterly subjective. Of course they're influenced by the opinions of others, the circumstances of life, the time of the month, the likely gain or loss, the last book read, or last sermon heard. Of course they're liable to self-delusion. But they're there, and they're powerful influencers.

Often I've been caught by surprise by that inner knowing. What I've felt deep down hasn't coincided with what looks possible, nor with what I'd naturally want to do. But a thought has taken hold with a real conviction that it's God's will.

A trusted friend asked me in confidence if I'd consider leaving the pastorate of my church and moving to another. It didn't make sense. The church where I was already ministering was about to open its own church building, the beginning, we hoped, of a great new phase of growth. The other church was in turmoil, didn't know me, and there was no reason to think I'd be the right person for them. But Alison and I prayed about it. We reckoned the idea would die at birth. It didn't. Within two days we felt strongly enough that there could be something in this that I had to phone my friend and say we were open to possibilities. He promised to pass on my name to the leaders of the pastoral vacancy committee. More and more the belief grew that God might well have something new planned for us.

But for months there was no contact from the other church. Then we heard, but it was grapevine talk, that they had someone else as their sole nominee to become minister. That didn't make sense to us. Sole nominees were virtually always accepted, so it must mean our inner leading was wrong. But the sole nominee wasn't accepted. The church had to look again. Eventually they asked me to preach. I preached, talked to their vacancy committee, and waited. They wrote. The answer was 'Thank you, but no. We don't feel you're the right person for us.' That didn't fit. It didn't match with what we believed. But by now we were having a great time in our present church with more conversions in six months than we'd seen in the previous six years. Our young church was growing fast. But the gut feeling that God wanted us elsewhere wouldn't go.

Eventually I talked to the friend who'd raised the possibility in the first place. 'I still feel drawn to that church,' I told him, 'but it looks impossible. Should I let the idea die?' 'I think you should,' he said. He knew the church was heading towards appointing another sole nominee. But for us, this was an idea that refused to die. We tried to put it out of our minds. We told God we were handing the issue over to him, but no matter how many times we gave it away we still had it.

Again, amazingly, the other congregation turned down a sole nominee. Two months later the church secretary phoned me. Their leadership had been at prayer, experienced a breath of God's Spirit upon them, confessed failure, and felt led to return to the stage where they believed they'd gone wrong and begin again from there. What that meant in practical terms was to talk further with me about the pastorate. We did. Six months later I was inducted as their minister, a role which lasted for more than ten years and was a good and important time of growth and change for everyone.

That's a sensitive personal story. I tell it to illustrate the mystery of simply knowing something deep inside. Alison and I could have been mistaken, and we were always willing to come to terms with that. Those who think themselves infallible in sensing God's will hurt themselves and often many others. Humility – being prepared to say 'I got it wrong' – is an essential quality. But as long as what we felt God wanted was possible, even when it looked impossible, we were willing to stay with it, pray for it, look for it. And it happened.

Gut feelings like that are often how people know they're called.

A sense of peace

Sometimes people feel right about one course of action and, correspondingly, not at all right about other options. They have an impression that God is with them in one possibility; he seems far away with other choices. They 'have a sense of peace' or 'have no peace'.

Like gut feelings, a sense of being at peace is highly subjective and seriously influenced by many things, especially what pleases or benefits us. I can be all too much at peace about something very wrong, and deeply uneasy about something very right. I often meet up with colleagues for an early-morning prayer meeting. When the alarm rings an hour before normal what would give me a sense of peace? Rolling over and shutting my eyes again. What disturbs my spirit? Getting up. Sure, if I did go back to sleep and missed the prayer meeting I'd feel bad, but not until later. At the time it would be wonderful.

So there must be the caution to define a sense of peace, not by what makes us feel good, but by what we know is right. A married couple with a baby daughter talked with me about whether or not God was calling them to do mission work in Afghanistan during the Russian occupation of the 1980s. Kabul was a dangerous place, and their work would take them right among the warring factions. Many thought them mad, especially with a young child. They knew the dangers. And they were frightened. But they found they could be at peace only by saying yes to going. And, for the years they were there, they kept that sense of peace in the midst of personal hardship and suffering all around them. They wouldn't have felt safe or felt right anywhere else.

'God spoke to me'

Some people seem to have a running conversation with God about everything. 'The new trousers had a broken zip, so I asked the Lord what to do and he said, "Take them back and get a refund." When I got there, the shop assistant looked glum, so I asked God if I should speak to him about Jesus, and God said, "Go for it." So I told him, "Your life is like these trousers with a broken zip. It just doesn't mesh together. It needs to be exchanged for a new life with everything functioning as it should." I don't know if I got through to him, but he certainly smiled when I told him that.' I'm sure he did.

I suspect many use 'God told me' language to mean what the rest of us call 'Here's what I think I should do'.

But there is a bigger scale and more important sense to the phrase 'God spoke to me' and it can apply to being called to mission. It's almost the easiest thing in the world to claim, and who can argue that God didn't? Sometimes it's so clear that we have no doubt what God wants; sometimes we wonder if we're making it up, hearing only what our imagination or ambition wants us to hear. But when you know God has spoken, it's life-changing.

In the previous chapter I described feeling led into Christian work. It was a great plan but I had no money for at least the first phase of study. I talked to respected friends, including some wise and important people in the church. One said, 'Whatever you do, don't give up your work until you know where the money is coming from for your studies.' It was sensible advice. I wrote countless letters to enquire about part-time jobs. Some replied saying they'd no vacancies. Many didn't bother answering. I asked around. Nothing. Critical dates were approaching fast, and I had to make a decision whether to apply for a college course. One night I sat writing to a friend, telling her I was getting nowhere with my search for part-time work. There were no jobs and no prospects for money from any other source. A lot of my weariness and confusion went into that letter.

Suddenly, as I sat pen in hand, my brain flooded with a complete thought, as if every part from beginning to end arrived simultaneously. 'Stop applying for jobs. Just trust me. I'll supply all you need.' The words couldn't be clearer. And I knew they were from God. How? I just knew. I got down on my knees, and said, 'God, I don't know how you can supply what I need, but I trust you.' And I did. I knew God had spoken. If he was calling me forward there would be a way. I sat back down at my table, and wrote to my friend that something very strange had just happened, that God had told me to trust him for money and get started with my studies. She must have thought I'd cracked under the strain, but I wish I had a copy of that letter now.

God speaks and when you know deep inside yourself he has, you can't help but listen.

> That night I could not get to sleep, but it seemed as though I heard someone say these words over and over, 'Ask of Me and I will give thee the heathen for thine inheritance, and the uttermost parts of the earth for thy possession.' I knew it was God's voice speaking to me, and that I had received my marching orders to go to China.
>
> C. T. Studd, *Cricketer and Pioneer*, Norman P. Grubb
> (The Religious Tract Society, 1933)

Coincidences

'It all came together. All on one day. My boss told me I was sacked, I wrote off my car, my wife said she was leaving me and taking the children, the cat got run over and the house burned down. That night, in the newspaper wrapping my Chinese takeaway, I saw this article about mission overseas. With all that had happened that day, I knew God was guiding me to be a missionary. I was suddenly free to serve him in a new way.'

All right, no-one has quite given me that story. But nearly. Lots of people find great significance in coincidences of circumstances and timing. A toned-down version of the above would be the person who sees an advert for mission work on the very day he hears his firm will be making him redundant. The timing is remarkable, and so he concludes this must be God's will.

It's hard not to be cynical. Unless, that is, we're honest enough to admit to occasions when we've read a meaning into certain things happening together, or met particular people at critical moments, or found something just when we needed to make a decision. Those haven't seemed ordinary, everyday occurrences. Happening just when they did was strangely important. We've believed God was showing us something, as he moved a number of chess pieces into place so that one particular strategy would work. We've seen and followed that plan and something good and important resulted. We were led. God guided us by coincidences.

The danger is not that of seeing God at work in unusual concurrences of timing or circumstance. The danger is unwarranted interpretations of them, when we find a meaning in events which owes more to our own wishes or imagination than some intrinsic significance in what's occurred.

Is God calling the man who has just lost his job and whose wife has left him to mission work at this time? I doubt it. He may see himself as free to serve God, but there are things in his life that need attention first. Sure, he read something about mission the same day he lost his wife, children, work, car, cat and home. But he had to use a bus that day. Does that mean he should be a bus driver? He ate his takeaway in a shop doorway, watching a programme about space exploration on the TV in the shop. Is God telling him to be an astronaut? Why was reading an article about mission significant rather than these? Maybe because he doesn't want to drive buses and maybe he knows he could never fly a space shuttle. Mission, he thinks, he could do. And it would make him feel his life was worthwhile at a time when he's lost so much that gave him a sense of worth. I feel sorry for him. I think he needs help, including finding a solid base for his self-worth. But I don't think his coincidences prove what he thinks they do.

Strange events which are more than coincidences happen. God uses them to get our attention and point us down a particular road. But sometimes we're too willing to be pointed in a particular way, and God is credited with more than God intended. Caution is needed.

***

Mrs Slessor never missed hearing those who came to Dundee, and once she was so much moved by an address from the Rev. William Anderson as to the needs of Old Calabar [in West Africa] that she longed to dedicate her son John to the work. He was a gentle lad, much loved by [his sister] Mary. Apprenticed to a blacksmith, his health began to fail, and a change of climate became imperative. He emigrated to New Zealand, but died a week after landing. His mother felt the blow to her hopes even more than his death. To Mary the event was a bitter grief, and it turned her thoughts more directly to the foreign field. Could she fill her brother's place? Would it be possible for her ever to become a missionary? The idea floated for a time through her mind, unformed and unconfessed, until it gradually resolved itself into a definite purpose.

W. P. Livingstone, writing about the call of Mary Slessor
Mary Slessor of Calabar (Hodder and Stoughton, 1915)

***

Fleeces

Bubbles of cynicism rise to the surface within many ministers when one of their congregation mentions setting out a fleece. The claim is to be acting like Gideon of old, asking God to clarify his will by making a certain sequence of events come to pass.

Gideon said to God, 'If you will save Israel by my hand as you have promised – look, I will place a wool fleece on the threshing-floor. If there is dew only on the fleece and all the ground is dry, then I will know that you will save Israel by my hand, as you said.' And that is what happened. Gideon rose early the next day; he squeezed the fleece and wrung out the dew – a bowlful of water.

Then Gideon said to God, 'Do not be angry with me. Let me make just one more request. Allow me one more test with the fleece. This time make the fleece dry and the ground covered with dew.' That night God did so. Only the fleece was dry; all the ground was covered with dew. (Judg. 6:36–40)

This wasn't unreasonable for Gideon. He'd heard God commission him to lead his embattled, dispirited nation against thousands of invading Midianites. It was a suicide mission. Unsurprisingly he felt the need to check out that what he'd heard was really God's will. This was not a moment for any misunderstanding. Likewise, when God's will isn't crystal-clear (which is usually), and when the issue really matters, we want to get it right. So we copy Gideon. Fleeces aren't too readily available to follow his method literally. But it's not difficult to devise some similar test. Maybe it could rain tomorrow at 3 o'clock. Maybe it could rain tomorrow at 3 o'clock and Aunt Mary phone five minutes later to say, 'Have you noticed it's raining?' Some short or long sequence of events is worked out. If it happens, that's a sign one way (usually positive, that some plan is right). If it doesn't, that's a sign the other way (probably that something shouldn't happen). It's up to God to make it clear.

And that's the big advantage of fleeces. It takes the heat off us and puts it on to God. No longer do I have to struggle with uncertainty, not sure whether to do this or that thing. If God wants option A he'd better make one set of events come about. If he wants option B he'd better make the other set happen. I don't have to weigh up factors, or discern God's leading. Here's a fleece. Let God make it happen or not, according to his will. The responsibility is his.

All that seems very spiritual. In fact it can be just the opposite. It can be a refusal to be a mature person with the courage to make a decision. And it can be a failure to be a mature Christian who'll walk by faith believing what God has already made clear. We can never avoid having to risk decisions and never avoid having to act in faith. Fleece setting runs the risk of doubting God. Gideon was certainly worried that God would get angry with him. No wonder. He was questioning what God had told him to do. Since a fleece is usually to confirm or refute a possible plan, often there will be a prior sense of God's will. There's a serious risk of trying to put God to the test.

Besides, there's the complication that there are some things we really want to happen, and other things we really don't want to happen. The fleece we lay out tends to be easy or difficult according to the result we want. Jean thinks there would be nothing more wonderful than marrying Frank. But Frank is going to be a missionary and wouldn't consider marrying anyone without the same call. So Jean defines her fleece. There must be an appeal for Christian nurses to work in the developing world in the very next magazine she reads. Sounds fair. Sounds difficult. No, it's not, for she fixes those conditions on Sunday morning knowing she'll collect her copy of the monthly mission magazine at church. That magazine comes from an agency dedicated solely to Christian medical work in the developing world, and in twenty years hasn't put out an edition without an appeal for more nurses to go there. Jean's fleece is a near guaranteed success. She gets her call and, she hopes, Frank too.

Conversely, it's not difficult to devise a set of circumstances so perverse that, while not impossible, God's omnipotence is definitely put on the line: 'If this call is right, let the hair grow back on my head, my bank account gain an anonymous donation of £100,000, and my Lada turn into a Ferrari.' The great thing about that kind of fleece is that when it doesn't work you escape what you never wanted to do anyway, and if somehow it does you get wonderful compensation for taking on a hard task.

Are fleeces wrong? No, but at least we ought to admit they're very uncommon biblically. Gideon's fleece is virtually the only example. Next nearest is the method used by Abraham's servant when he was sent to find a wife for Isaac. He prayed that when he asked girls for water to drink the right one would not only give him a drink but offer to water his camels too (Gen. 24:14). It worked. God used it to lead him to Rebekah. She was clearly a kind, hospitable young woman. The fact that she was also a stunning beauty was probably not irrelevant, especially for Isaac. Supposing she'd been disadvantaged in the beauty stakes, and suppose Isaac had asked the servant, 'Why did you choose her?' and been told, 'Well, she's very caring for camels . . . ,' would he have been convinced by the servant's method of getting guidance? Perhaps not. But the method brought God's choice, *and* she was beautiful. Isaac was happy – 'he loved her' (Gen. 24:67).

Fleeces – fixed sequences of events to show God's will – can turn out well. But the practice isn't frequent in Scripture, and probably shouldn't dominate as a way of getting guidance or checking out a sense of call. Yes, God answers fleece-type prayers. But the danger is using them to avoid the responsibility of making a decision, abandoning ourselves by a prayer to whichever way a set of circumstances works out. It can be spiritual coin-flipping. More often God calls us to make choices in faith.

Scripture verses

I've known people for whom every major decision rested on guidance from a Scripture verse which had 'leaped out at them' or been whispered in their ears by the Holy Spirit. At worst, their book of daily readings became a spiritual horoscope. At best, they were in danger of lifting a sentence from the Bible right out of context and applying its meaning to their lives uncritically.

Yet there are moments when particular verses of the Bible can be remarkably pertinent, A friend broke off with his girlfriend on the basis of reading Jeremiah 16:1–2 ('Then the word of the LORD came to me: "You must not marry and have sons or daughters in this place" '). I suspect he may have felt the relationship had already outlived its romance, but he was glad of what he saw as confirmation.

It's not unreasonable that people open their Bibles for help when they're not sure what God wants. They see the Bible as 'God's word', so expect verses or whole passages to 'speak' to them, not just in general terms but when they need specific guidance. Often they get it. I have. I wrote earlier how I sensed God telling me to leave journalism and go ahead with study for ministry, even though I had no idea where funds could come from for at least the first part of my studies. That Sunday there was a guest preacher in church. He knew nothing of my situation. The passage he spoke on was Matthew 6:25–34. It begins, 'Therefore I tell you, do not worry about your life, what you will eat or drink; or about your body, what you will wear' (v. 25). In the middle it says, 'If that is how God clothes the grass of the field, which is here today and tomorrow is thrown into the fire, will he not much more clothe you, O you of little faith?' (v. 30) And near the end it says, 'But seek first his kingdom and his righteousness, and all these things will be given to you as well' (v. 33). Those words, right at the time of launching out on my biggest faith journey to date, were immensely significant. It felt like God was reassuring me, and within days I'd handed in my resignation. God's guidance isn't for amusement or interest, but for action.

But the Bible is abused when odd verses are extracted and made to mean something different from what's original or natural. 'Fight the good fight' (1 Tim. 6:12) cannot legitimately be construed as a call to take up boxing, nor 'I was delivered from the lion's mouth' (2 Tim. 4:17) as guidance to be a lion-tamer. Likewise, finding the verse 'You will be his witness to all men of what you have seen or heard' (Acts 22:15) in your daily reading is not proof by itself that God means you to be an internationally renowned evangelist.

God will use the Bible to call people to service. But it won't generally be by gilt-edging isolated texts. It'll be by helping them understand God's love for the lost and knowing the right priorities for their lives.

Getting a sign

I've learned two things about signs. One, they're uncommon when you don't want them but remarkably plentiful when you really want them. Two, they're rarely of the quality of moving stars resting over stables, bushes that burn without being consumed or donkeys that enter into conversation with you.

When signs are numerous I suspect I'm guilty of wishful thinking. The low-key nature of most signs makes me realise, yet again, that there's usually more than one interpretation that can be placed on them.

Signs happen, though. Money arrives unexpectedly, making a previously impossible project possible. A friend says something with a relevance and significance far greater than she could have known. There's a dream with special meaning, or a rainbow in the sky at a special moment. A sign could be a healing, or a death, or a pregnancy, or a failed exam, or a promotion at work, or an offer of early retirement, and so on. Sometimes what's special is the event. Sometimes it's the circumstances in which the event happens. Sometimes it's both.

Alison and I were unsure whether or not God was calling us to Craigmillar, a huge housing complex on the edge of Edinburgh. The place ranked high for problems. It had few rivals in league tables for squalor, violence, theft, drug abuse, poverty, dysfunctional families, poor school performance, and numbers waiting to be rehoused elsewhere. We'd been looking for some time for another place to live, viewing various properties but without success. Was God now calling us to this run-down area? We doubted it. With a son a year old, and optimism about a companion for him in another year, it didn't seem a wise choice. We prayed, but kept looking elsewhere. Finally we found a home in a more respectable area of the city. The usual practice was to make an offer for a property and then wait to see if it was accepted. But this house was for sale on a fixed-price basis. All we had to do was offer to pay that price. We did. Unthinkably our offer was refused; the owner decided he wanted more. We had to back out. That experience pulled us up short. We'd been looking for ages. Nothing was working out, and now what should have been a definite deal had failed. What was God doing with us? We moved to Craigmillar. The 'sign' was modest, but its effect on us was far-reaching.

I'd love to have huge signs telling me what to do. Letters 200 feet high against a cloudless sky would be fine. Or words suddenly appearing on a blank computer screen. Maybe that would be the modern equivalent of the apostle Paul's sign when he had a vision of a man of Macedonia begging him to evangelise there (Acts 16:9–10). But there are big signs I wouldn't fancy. Some have written books about how their lives have been redirected after experiences of 'dying' and then returning to this world. I think that would redirect most people's lives, but it would be a high-risk strategy just to get a sign.

Prophecies

In the Bible, directive prophecies were quite often the way someone was guided. Paul was told by Ananias: 'The God of our fathers has chosen you to know his will and to see the Righteous One and to hear words from his mouth. You will be his witness to all men of what you have seen and heard' (Acts 22:14–15). David's selection or call to be the next King of Israel was prophecy by action rather than words, but it certainly marked out the young man: 'So Samuel took the horn of oil and anointed him in the presence of his brothers, and from that day on the Spirit of the LORD came upon David in power' (1 Sam. 16:13). Sometimes a prophecy merely explained part of what's involved, like the prophetic actions and words of Agabus to Paul: 'After we had been there a number of days, a prophet named Agabus came down from Judea. Coming over to us, he took Paul's belt, tied his own hands and feet with it and said, "The Holy Spirit says, 'In this way the Jews of Jerusalem will bind the owner of this belt and will hand him over to the Gentiles' " ' (Acts 21:10–11).

To some degree, all these are prophecies which direct someone's life. That can still happen. The profoundly scary thing is the risk of getting it wrong or of downright abuse. If I had a strong belief that what my town needed was a centre for drop-outs, I might find it all too easy to speak a prophecy directing a newly converted millionaire to get involved in the project. My motives might be entirely good (or not!), but the danger of shaping God's will by my words would be high.

Even where there's no self-interest for the prophet I'm frightened by the implications for those hearing the prophecy. The whole of life can be turned upside down by one sentence spoken on behalf of God. At a large meeting, I listened while people stood, and someone who didn't know them pronounced God's will for their lives. One was told he'd have an international youth ministry which would be very successful globally in drawing young people to Christ. I watched the young man drink this prophecy in, deeply wanting to serve God. I imagined him handing in his resignation from work, and starting out on this ministry on the strength of that prophecy. I don't know what happened. Maybe he's being greatly used. Hopefully the prophet didn't get it wrong. But that was high-risk territory.

God calls people by prophecies. There's no reason why he can't put the right words into someone's mouth that will guide them to new forms of Christian work. The method is simple because it's direct. Because it's direct it's also hazardous. Wise people check out prophecies against other criteria (including some listed here), and especially with trusted friends and spiritual leaders. Very few prophecies should be believed that fly in the face of their advice.

Visions, voices, dreams, drawing lots, instructions from angels

There are biblical examples of all these, and plenty more strange and supernatural methods by which people have sensed God's call. There's an attraction about them. Some people prefer their guidance to be as weird as possible, the weirder the better, for it makes them all the more sure God must have brought it to pass. But it isn't that simple. I've dreamed some positively bizarre dreams but they were a tribute to my imagination and not to God's guidance. I've had some great visions but they owed more to my wishful thinking than divine revelation.

There are no unambiguous signs, nothing that sweeps all doubt away. Even a bush that burned without being consumed didn't persuade Moses that he ought to rush to Egypt and get about God's work. He doubted, questioned and argued. The task was huge, and the potential for loss immense. God's will seems crystal-clear to us as we read the record now, but we have the luxury of being dispassionate. Moses was being asked to demand freedom for slaves, an impossible and hostile request, and to do so in a country from which he'd fled because he'd committed murder. Under these circumstances, not even God's voice out of a burning bush was overwhelming guidance.

Gideon's response was similar. He should never have needed to lay out a fleece. He'd already had meat and bread instantly consumed by fire, and a conversation with an angel who suddenly disappeared. These were not normal events in Gideon's life. You'd think he'd be sure what God wanted. He knew, but he wasn't a hundred per cent certain. Maybe they were powerful signs, but of what? Suppose he'd misunderstood? Or hallucinated? He had to check.

We can be grateful for any strange events that show what God wants. But there are many factors which influence how we respond to any signs. Some are desperate for a change in their lives and will latch on to the flimsiest evidence as being important guidance. Others feel they or their family have much to lose by any change, and their first reaction is to discount anything that disturbs the status quo. Maybe the critical question is not how weird our guidance is. Maybe what matters is how willing we are to let God do the guiding for our lives.

Sanctified common sense

Here are three statements.

- We can be so preoccupied looking for special dramatic guidance that we miss boring, plain indicators of what's right.
- We can be so convinced that God demands the extraordinary that we fail to do what's obvious.
- I can do many things that everyone can do; what's right for me will often be what no-one else can do.

Those three statements won't please my hyperspiritual friends who seem to need revelations and signs before they'll believe anything is God's will, who seem convinced that God always has bigger and more exciting work than what blatantly needs doing, and who don't value ideas or plans that have been worked out logically.

But the truth is that there aren't always signs. The mundane but important things of this world are God's will too. And brainpower is part of God's gifting of his children and not to be despised.

Betty longed to serve God. If only she could get some kind of revelation of what God wanted her to do. Was it a healing ministry? What about counselling? Maybe she was meant to really launch out and care for the poor and lonely in Asia? Betty spent hours in prayer, wishing God would make his will known. Her prayers were interrupted one day by police cars outside her neighbour's house. Then there was an ambulance, but it left ominously slowly. Betty heard eventually what it was all about. It appears that the old lady next door had died. The really sad thing was that she had been dead for a month and no-one knew. 'Someone ought to have cared for her,' Betty said to herself, and went back to praying for God to reveal how she should serve him.

We can miss the obvious and bypass common sense all so easily when we're seeking guidance.

Given an all-too-manic lifestyle, the last of the three statements has come to mean much to me. If I had time and energy for ten tasks, and there were only ten tasks to be done, life would be simple. But usually I am in a situation where I have time and energy for ten tasks but see one hundred and ten to be done. I can't do them all. How do I choose?

'Pray about it,' I'm told. Certainly, but there's also nothing unspiritual about using simple logic. There are many of those hundred and ten tasks I'm not able to do. I can't rewire a house, drive a bus, remove an appendix, or many other things requiring specialised skills I don't have. So they're not right for me. Probably half the possibilities disappear immediately. Of the fifty-five remaining, most are tasks that lots of people can do. They're general duties, the kind that most folk are good at, perhaps driving someone to hospital, washing dishes, setting out chairs, giving someone a meal. I could do these, and do them well. But there are also a few tasks that fit with my training and my skills especially. A sermon has to be preached, an article has to be written, a management issue needs attention, and several more. I may be the only one around at that time who can do those things. In that situation I don't need to pray for very long to know which ten tasks out of the one hundred and ten are the right ones for me. God wants me to do the things for which he's given me particular gifting.

Issues like these are directly relevant when it comes to a call to mission. There are moments in life when all circumstances combine to make mission service possible. Money, health, family situation, work skills and other factors are all in place. The bias is towards going ahead, and that should not be ignored. Or there's a gap that we are uniquely suited to fill, like a nursing friend who had exactly the right professional experience to take the place of someone in a mission hospital so that she could go home for rest. She was the right person with the right skills at the right time. She would have needed guidance *not* to go.

Common-sense principles like these can also be used as an indicator that there *isn't* a special call to mission. C. H. Spurgeon, a famous preacher of the second half of the nineteenth century, founded his own college for training pastors. One guideline he used in selecting who could be enrolled for training was a person's ability to speak sufficiently loudly. In days before amplification, voice projection was vital. Someone whose lung power wasn't strong simply wasn't called into the ministry, he reckoned. Likewise, a person with chronically poor health probably isn't called to serve God in a country which would exacerbate the condition. Nor is someone without a gift for preaching in their own culture suddenly going to develop the gift when communicating cross-culturally. Nor is someone with major family responsibilities in their home country, which only he or she can fulfil, likely to be called overseas at that time. Sometimes we miss the obvious when we're looking for guidance.

Dangers

There are two special dangers to watch out for when trying to work out whether or not God is calling us to a special role in mission.

One is filling a vacuum in our lives. Everyone longs for fulfilment and a major way in which Christians are fulfilled is by knowing their lives are useful to God. So, when a course of education, a career, or even a marriage isn't working out, life feels empty and purposeless. What would change that feeling? Nothing could do it better than to serve God full-time. Deep psychological and spiritual needs predispose some people to find a call from God to Christian work. Often they believe God wants them to be missionaries. Then they'd be really useful, serving God, extending his kingdom. Even the fact that other areas of life haven't worked out is interpreted as 'God closing the door' to those things to leave it open for mission. The call can seem convincing. Spurgeon wasn't persuaded when people with a story like that applied for admission to his ministers' college. He reckoned that anyone able to succeed in ministry could probably succeed in six other professions as well. Many whose careers are getting nowhere have approached me with a sense of call to Christian service at home or overseas. Some are out of work, others stuck in dead-end jobs. I don't turn them down flat. But I suggest they take longer checking out their guidance. And, if they can move to a healthy work situation which offers a good career path, I urge them to make that move and then see if they still feel called.

The other danger has to do with spiritualising our wants. Full-time Christian work is very attractive to many people. To be a minister or missionary is to be at the front line for God, to enter a new dimension of holiness, to relate to God at a depth unavailable to others, to sacrifice without thought to the cost. Ministers and missionaries don't see it that way, but from the days of the first-century apostles people have romanticised what it's like to work for God full-time. Once people want something badly enough it's not difficult to find circumstances and signs that point them in that direction. Some have said, 'I'll go ahead with an application to a Bible college, and I'll know it's right if they accept me.' At the risk of disparaging the entry procedures to Bible colleges, these people fail to realise that some colleges are predisposed to accept new students unless they're singularly unsuited to the course or college life. Acceptance should not be equated with proof of call. But often it is for the person who sincerely wants to be called.

I wish all work was seen as full-time Christian work. I wish every work-place, every neighbourhood, every home was seen as a mission field. I wish every church was a mission force. I wish our eyes were opened to the spiritual warfare we fight every day. I wish we saw and took every day's opportunities to serve God. I wish we had a sense of achieving something important for God, of advancing his kingdom, of doing things of eternal importance. If those wishes came true, there'd be no need to romanticise one form of Christian work and less danger of self-generating a call to mission out of a need to be doing something that matters.

All dangers can't be avoided. There are no infallible ways to avoid false guidance. But I have three final tests of a sense of call.

One Do those who know you well enough to be ruthlessly honest with you agree that you're called? (That should include your wife or husband!)

Two Does the work to which you feel called fit with the way God has been using you until now? (Gifts that weren't there before don't suddenly get invented just because you become a mission worker.)

Three Has this sense of call lasted? (I'm more persuaded about a sense of call that's been there for a winter and summer than one that just appeared one dull autumn day of life.)

By faith or by sight?

Paul wrote, 'We live by faith, not by sight' (2 Cor. 5:7), but we'd rather reverse that. We crave certainty. We don't want to leave what's familiar and makes us feel safe, unless it's definite that what we're going to is exactly what God wants and preferably that it will make us happy. If we are to give up our present security we need to know that big decision is precisely right, especially if we're making sacrifices and if the choice is irreversible. We'd like to be really sure.

In that case, we'll never do anything. To want sureness is understandable but unattainable. We can't have any certainty greater than that of Matthew who had to walk away from his tax-collecting, or Peter and Andrew from their fishing. Yes, they had Jesus's face-to-face call, but how could they be *sure* he wasn't a crackpot preacher whose promises meant nothing? They had to trust the call they felt in their hearts as well as heard in their ears, and then go forward swallowing down whatever doubts remained.

It won't be different for any of us. Of course we should know as well as we can know, but calls are messy things and there's no way to clean them up. If only we could measure every sense of leading against a certainty rating. Police can use a lie detector; why can't we have a call detector? We could input our signs, or measure our spiritual goose bumps, and get a score. Anything above eighty per cent would be enough to be sure God was behind the call.

We'll never have a call detector. We'll always have some questions, always some fears, always some uncertainty. Maybe it's part of God's plan to keep us looking to him for help, and finding our real security in our relationship with him.

Real courage isn't feeling no fear or having no doubts. Real courage is being frightened and unsure but going forward anyway. It's saying, 'God, I'm still scared. All my fears aren't gone, and I don't know your will for certain, but I believe this is what you want from me, so I trust you.'

If that point has been reached honestly and prayerfully, God honours it. It's been the position of virtually every Christian missionary that's ever lived. And God has poured his power on weak people like them and done some remarkable things through them. There's no reason it'll be any different with the scared but brave people he calls today.

Chapter 8

Why are some good at doing mission?

IT'S A HARD truth. Some are good at sharing the gospel with others and some aren't. Some get into conversations on spiritual topics, seem to find chances to share God's love, get things done to make the world a different place, and people come to faith through their witness. Often others don't see any of that.

Sally was always talking about the Lord with someone. Her neighbours all knew she was a Christian, and so did the assistant in the baker's shop down the road. Sally told them what she was praying for, or what had happened at church that Sunday, or how wonderful it was that a friend had been healed. As far as I was concerned these were conversations with a high cringe factor. I reckoned everyone would take fright. They didn't. Sure, some never got further than nodding politely, but others asked Sally questions, often quite deep questions. More than a few shared their problems with her. Here was someone who listened, who cared, whose faith really meant something to her, and who was interested in them without trying to sell them anything. They trusted her. Here and there people came to faith in Christ through Sally's witness.

Why was Sally good at mission? Why not everyone? Was she gifted for evangelism while others aren't? There are people called by God to be evangelists (Eph. 4:11), but nothing about Sally smacked of anyone special. She was just an ordinary Christian who was extraordinarily good at helping other people experience the love of God.

What is it, then, that makes some people good at doing mission? Is it inbred, an innate ability to pass on the faith? Or could all of us be better at it?

There are lessons all of us can learn, but they're remarkably basic. They're not things that require courses to be passed or conferences to be attended. They are common-sense, basic Christian principles put into practice.

Witness gets done

The number one reason why some are so much better at mission than others is that they do it. They actually share their faith. When they meet people who don't know Jesus they tell them. When they find folk with deep needs in their lives they help. When they see wrongs they put them right. They don't just theorise about God's work, they do it.

Put two people side by side. One is a brand-new Christian. She's hardly known Jesus for any time at all, hasn't read all the New Testament, doesn't understand words like atonement, predestination or premillennialism, has never done a course on evangelism, and still thinks the minister's sermons are brilliant teaching about God. Next to her is the 'Thirty years since I gave my life to Jesus' Christian. She's used all the Bible study guides, done all the courses, can give five different theories of the atonement, three of election, and six about the events of the Parousia (and even knows what that means). Frankly, she reckons most of the sermons she hears are beneath her.

On average, which is the better witness? Almost always it's the brand-new Christian. It shouldn't be. She hasn't a fraction of the knowledge, training or experience of her neighbour in the pew. But she leads people to Christ and the older Christian doesn't.

There are several explanations why that's usually how it is, and some are in the pages that follow. But there are two fundamental reasons.

First, the new Christian still knows non-Christians. They have been her whole world until now: family, friends, neighbours, people in the pub, colleagues at work, friends at the club. Literally dozens of people she talks to have never heard the message that God loves them, Jesus died for them, and that he wants to give them new lives and new hope. And every one of them sees the change in her life. Old habits and attitudes and maybe even some problems have gone. New ways, new joy, new love have come. Many would like what she's got. Everyone wants to know what made the difference.

That brings us to the second reason for her effectiveness. The new Christian tells her non-Christian friends what's made the difference. She shares the gospel. Perhaps her explanation is a bit basic. Perhaps she's a bit aggressive. Perhaps what she says isn't quite correct. But they're willing to hear and she doesn't hesitate to tell. After all, her logic goes, I may not know much but it was enough for me to become a Christian, so it'll be enough for them too. Often it is.

Our longer-in-the-tooth Christian isn't like the newcomer. Almost all the people she's close to are already Christians. No wonder. Sunday she's at church, Monday at leaders' meeting, Tuesday she's preparing her Sunday School class, Wednesday is home group, Thursday she helps with the youth club, Friday she rehearses with the choir, and Saturday is either a special event at church or a chance to collapse in front of the telly and get away from everyone for an evening. She hasn't time for neighbours. They'd get in the way of her doing her Christian work.

Besides, she's still searching for the right way to witness. She wants to share her faith. She believes Jesus is the only way to heaven, and feels guilty that she doesn't do more about evangelism. So every time she hears that there's a new course which will turn her into a super-evangelist for Jesus she signs up. She fits it into her busy schedule somehow, and week by week she studies how to make contacts, what the core gospel message is, how to share her testimony, and answers to difficult questions. She's done six courses like that. But not one of them has taken away the excruciating embarrassment she knows she'd feel at speaking about Jesus to the person who works across the office from her. She can't cope with that. So she keeps quiet.

The brand-new Christian hasn't learned the great secret of so many older Christians: we pray about witnessing, talk about witnessing, and learn about witnessing, but we don't actually do it. The new Christian realises she's discovered the most fantastic good news, tells everyone, and a remarkably high number of others believe too.

Opportunity is missed by most people because it is dressed in overalls and looks like work.

Thomas Edison (1847–1931)

People get close to those they want to reach

If, 2000 years ago, all God had wanted to do was give mankind a message, he could have done it without sending Jesus to earth. The incarnation wasn't necessary merely to pass on information. God had safer, faster, less pricy options. He might have painted words across the sky or drawn them in the dust of the earth. Or he could have dropped tracts from heaven. Or he could have pointed a loudspeaker through the clouds and blasted earth with words.

If he'd done any of those, we'd have read or heard his words at a superficial level but that's all. There are things that need a level of communication far greater than words if they are to be understood. A loving look or loving touch often speaks more eloquently than the finest vocabulary. God wanted to reach us at the greatest depth, to affect us body, mind and spirit. If all he'd done was throw words at us we wouldn't have known what he was really saying.

For that, Jesus had to be born. It couldn't be done with anything less than God's presence right with us. So Jesus came as one of us, speaking, touching, helping, caring, dying. There wasn't an inch of distance between God and humanity. He identified with us utterly. Then we began to understand God.

Effective mission will always have that depth of engagement about it. It'll mean real involvement between people. It can't be done at a distance. It means getting close to others. We bring the love of God in us alongside those who need that love, and let it get infectious.

It's not 'safe' to live like that. Often I feel I must protect myself from those who'll drain me of energy and time. I don't want to get sucked in to the endless and impossible problems of others. I'd rather not risk the emotional pain that's always part of real empathy with someone else's hurts. My instinct is to help at arm's length. Touch-and-run love.

But real mission is an embrace of love, not a fleeting touch. It's awkward, inconvenient, costly, risky. There's pain, sacrifice, weariness, weakness, sometimes even death. But love like that changes lives.

I was twenty-two and on a mission team trying to convert youngsters in a huge Aberdeen housing complex. We visited homes, led meetings in the local school, called on contacts, and each evening ran a coffee bar in the church hall. The coffee bar pandered to the egos of some of us. Arrogant show-offs that we were, we strummed our guitars and sang, performed drama, or stood up at the front and preached full of passion and witticisms. We knew how to put over the gospel to that generation. We reckoned it very impressive. Of course, not everyone on the mission team was a singer, actor or preacher. One young woman had none of these up-front gifts and sometimes wondered where she fitted in. So she did the only thing she could, and looked for a youngster in the coffee bar who was on her own. She found twelve-year-old Arlene, a shy girl who hid beneath a bright red mop of curly hair. Arlene was so quiet, no-one had ever managed to get a whole sentence out of her, and she'd been left to sit alone. But this team member accepted Arlene was like that, and simply kept her company. By the end of the evening there were a few words.

Arlene was back the next night. Most of us were too busy for her. Singing, performing, speaking were time-consuming things. Thankfully the same mission team member saw her, sat with her through the whole coffee bar time, chatting a little more than the night before. So it went on through a whole week. Arlene came back night after night. The team member gave her friendship and companionship while the rest of us strutted proudly at the front. At the end of that week, some of us reckoned we'd done a great job putting over the gospel, and we looked for a harvest of conversions among those who had hung around the front watching us perform. There wasn't one. No-one at all was converted. Except Arlene. Simply, hesitantly she had asked Jesus to take control of her life. Each evening the same team member had sat quietly with her at the back of the hall, taking an interest in her life, listening to her dreams. That had meant a lot to her. And Arlene became a Christian, the only youngster that week to make a decision for Christ. I learned something from that team member about getting alongside people and not merely shouting the gospel at a distance. Actually, over the years I've learned a lot from that team member. I was so impressed I married her.

People are people, not spiritual scalps

My friend had suggested we spend an evening together. Sounded great to me. We lounged in armchairs, chatting and sipping coffee. Then he said to me, 'What do you most want to have in life?' Quite a question! He didn't usually ask anything so deep. I murmured something about pleasing God, finding fulfilment, and a few more dreadfully pious things. 'Yes, but name some things you'd like to have if only you had the money to buy them.' I looked blank. I couldn't really think of anything. Besides, why was he asking? We staggered along a bit further in the conversation before he said, 'Tonight I'm going to show you a wonderful business opportunity so you can have all the things you ever wanted . . .'

As I heard those words, the penny dropped. I felt used. I was getting a sales pitch to become the next trader down the line from my friend so he could extend his own business. To be fair, he really believed he was doing me a favour, and our relationship has lasted way beyond the fact that he tried to enrol me and I refused to be enrolled. But it hurt that he hadn't wanted my time that evening for friendship. He wanted to be with me to build his business.

I've often wondered since then if that's how some have felt when I tried to share my faith with them. When I've said, 'Our church cares for you,' do people think, 'He just wants to fill his church,' or 'They must be needing money to repair their steeple'? When I've offered, 'We'd like to help you,' do they think, 'Sure, to believe what you believe and become one of your Christian club'? If they do, I can warble on about God and Jesus but they've already switched off because they reckon I'm only out to sell something and it's not something they want to buy.

We live in a suspicious and cynical world. Exploitation is a worldwide phenomenon, and the number of innocents declines every year. Marketing the gospel doesn't work, for these days most people spot and resist sales talk by halfway through the first sentence. Not only do they resist; sometimes they're offended that anyone tried to sign them up for Christianity.

But it doesn't have to be like that, and shouldn't be like that. Selling the gospel is unworthy. It's unworthy of Christ and un-worthy of those on the receiving end. Jesus is not the latest and best consumer commodity. Sure, knowing him is good for people, but Jesus is not to be offered as if he is the bargain of the week. He is Creator, Ruler, Saviour. He bled and died for all people. He rose from the grave and rules supreme. We don't package him and market him. We speak of him with gratitude, and share news of him with the passion of people rescued from the jaws of death telling others how they can escape too. Those we tell matter. They're not just lost souls who need our salvation product. They're mothers, sons, husbands, friends, colleagues, people with feelings, concerns, ambitions, ideas, abilities. In other words, from richest to poorest, from furthest east to furthest west, people are of value. They have status in God's creation. They're loved by him. His Son died for them. We don't collect conversion decisions as a salesman tallies clinched deals. We help men and women like ourselves find life. That doesn't offend. When people know they're cared for, they listen and often they respond.

Tom and Judith chose to live in one of South America's most volatile countries. It was a dangerous place to be a Christian. Openly disagreeing with the government meant a late-night visit from dark figures and a journey from which no-one ever returned. Churches were always under surveillance. They brought people together, virtually a subversive activity in itself from the point of view of the secret police. And they sided with the oppressed. Sometimes Christians found their names were on a death list, and courageous friends helped them vanish from that place. There are plenty of other countries in the world where Tom and Judith could have gone. All of them were places which needed their talents, places where they could serve God and be risk-free and comfortable. But they decided to live among frightened and threatened people. 'Even if we never do anything else, we want to stand with them through this time,' they said. What Tom and Judith did by living there mattered more than any speech by a foreign politician in his parliament or any pronouncement of judgment from a preacher in his pulpit, each thousands of miles away. My friends loved these people enough to share their risks. It's not surprising that many came to believe in their God.

Communicating in ways people understand

> 'Young man, if I thought I could win one more soul for Christ by standing on my head and beating a tambourine with my feet I would learn how to do it.'
>
> Words said to have been spoken by William Booth to Rudyard Kipling when the latter said he didn't like tambourines

Missiologists write about 'contextualisation' or even 'inculturation'. Posh words, but what they mean is telling the gospel in ways that make sense for the hearer.

There's a big difference between the world of the high-flying Wall Street stockbroker, only in his late twenties but already with two children, two cars, two homes and two marriages, and the destitute woman whose only belongings are scraps of clothes as she ekes out an existence on the pavement of Calcutta, the place where she was born, where she's given birth to all her children, and where she will live until disease claims her body at an appallingly early age. Apart from premature death – one from having too much of the things of this world and the other from having too little – they have next to nothing in common. They might as well be on different planets.

Both have needs but (apart from the ultimate need of all people to be right with God) they're not the same. One needs a runaway lifestyle arrested. The other needs food, clothing, shelter and hope for a better future. Can the gospel address both? Yes, but differently for each. Perhaps what the stockbroker needs to hear is the parable of the fool who made himself rich with things and neglected God (Luke 12:16–21). Maybe he'll realise his spiritual emptiness and turn to Christ. Perhaps without creating dependency and tempting her to profess faith for handouts, the impoverished woman needs people who'll be concerned for her physical well-being, who'll bring divine love to her pavement. She also needs to hear of a Saviour who welcomes people from all castes and nationalities and promises them an eternal inheritance. Maybe she'll be drawn to one who gives her hope for something beyond her present misery. Exactly how each of the people in these examples would be helped isn't important. The point is that each is different, and the gospel has to be presented to each of them differently. They must hear of the Christ who meets *their* needs. They must have a gospel applied to their 'world'.

> Holistic evangelism means that we take the situation in which people are – the situation which bothers them, which constantly affects their lives – and show how the Gospel and Jesus are relevant in and to their situation.
>
> Vinay Samuel and Chris Sugden
> 'Evangelism and Development', *New Frontiers in Mission*,
> Patrick Sookhdeo (ed.) (Paternoster Press, 1987)

Those who are good at mission never forget that. They scratch where people are itching, not where they think people ought to be itching. I visited Christians in Los Angeles who had an effective outreach programme to the gay and lesbian community. They were in contact with many from the hard-nosed, aggressive side of the gay scene. Their lifestyles were colourful and shocking. Most Christians I know would have had every moral nerve shrieking condemnation. If they'd got past being judgmental, they might have tried to share the gospel as a cure for guilt. The Christians in the outreach programme didn't present it that way. Didn't they believe a homosexual lifestyle was wrong? Yes, but they knew the gay men and women didn't think that. Those they wanted to reach weren't struggling with a sense of immorality but many *were* struggling with finding meaningful and lasting relationships. So that was the issue with which the Christians began, helping those who wanted love and security to find it in a God who cared for them and would never leave them. Presenting the gospel effectively takes account of the needs of those who are hearing it.

It also takes account of *how* it's presented.

My friend Martin learned that the hard way. He was invited to preach while on a trip to Brazil. He picked one of his best sermons, a message that had gone down a storm back home in Britain. He walked confidently to the pulpit. 'I'm going to speak about faith,' he began. The missionary translating into Portuguese for him nodded approvingly. Good topic. 'Faith is spelled F-A-I-T-H,'

Martin continued, 'which stands for Forsaking All I Trust Him.' The words flowed confidently from Martin but there was stunned silence from the translator. Eventually he whispered, 'That doesn't work in Portuguese.' 'Well, just make the best of it you can,' Martin said, and carried on enthusiastically using each of the capital letters of the English word 'faith'. It was a great sermon. But not in Portuguese.

What Martin did parallels what many of us do when speaking to non-Christians. We tell people what we think they should know, using our familiar words and ideas, and then blame them for not being interested or not understanding. Those who are good at mission don't do that. They don't assume others should adjust; they make themselves flexible.

Paul understood that, and maybe that's why he was such a good evangelist.

> Though I am free and belong to no man, I make myself a slave to everyone, to win as many as possible. To the Jews I became like a Jew, to win the Jews. To those under the law I became like one under the law (though I myself am not under the law), so as to win those under the law. To those not having the law I became like one not having the law (though I am not free from God's law but am under Christ's law), so as to win those not having the law. To the weak I became weak, to win the weak. I have become all things to all men so that by all possible means I might save some. I do all this for the sake of the gospel, that I may share in its blessings. (1 Cor. 9:19–23)

Paul was clearly no arrogant 'take it or leave it' preacher. If he had to change to get alongside his hearer, then he changed. He expected to speak to them on their terms; he did not expect them to listen to him on his terms.

Near the church where I was pastor, an unlet shop became available to us for a month. We decided we'd run it as a coffee shop, and see if we could get alongside folk in the area we never normally met, the kind who wouldn't think to enter the door of a church building. We weren't in the smart end of the city centre and coming into a large, impressive church building was a sizeable cultural barrier many couldn't cross easily. Large and impressive were not the words that sprang to mind when we surveyed the shop we were going to use. It wasn't in pristine condition. Since we would have it for only a month, we couldn't do much about the decor except drape a few banners and put up a few posters. Half a dozen borrowed tables and chairs were arranged in the main area, and someone had the idea of selling second-hand goods from a counter over to one side. No-one knew what to charge for either our merchandise or the coffee, but since the place didn't look all that great and we were interested not in making money but in meeting people we made it really cheap.

The response was fantastic. Before we opened on the first morning there was a queue at the door – they wanted to see if there were any bargains among our sale items. Once they'd checked them all, and found out how little it cost for a cup of tea or coffee, they sat down at one of the tables. And so it went on for the whole month. There were countless conversations and great contacts with people we would never have known otherwise. But it wouldn't have worked if we'd had more time or money to invest in that project. If it had been a long-term venture we'd have been tempted to smarten the place up. Then it wouldn't have fitted into the neighbourhood. We'd probably have employed someone to run it, so we'd have had to charge a more normal price for the hot drinks. That would have meant few in that area could have afforded them. Our café worked because it was right for that community. A different style of shop just wouldn't have been their kind of place.

Whether it's how the gospel is applied, the context in which the gospel is shared or the words used to share it, those who are good at mission communicate in ways that work for those on the receiving end. They talk their talk. They don't use *Times* language for *Mirror* readers. They get into other people's worlds, bring the gospel to bear on the needs those people have, and express it in ways they can receive and understand.

They don't say, 'Become like me'

I visited a village deep in a secluded valley in North Thailand. Virtually everyone who lived there was a Christian, some of them people who'd been rejected elsewhere but found a welcome and safety in that village. I shook hands with a man who was once a murderer but was now changed and a leader among the people. It was a village without many comforts, but the people lived in harmony and peace.

Only one thing saddened me, and it was when they showed me their church. They were proud of the building, built on the highest bit of land in the village because, for Thais, height equals importance and no building was more important than their church. It was a simple structure, really just a rectangular, open-sided frame with a corrugated tin roof and a small platform at the end. My heart sank at the one other thing under that roof: pews. Row upon row of wooden benches faced forwards. In home after home in that village I'd squatted on boards or bamboo matting on the floor because Thai villagers don't sit on chairs. But when they'd built their church they'd put pews in it. I don't know where they'd got the idea from, but someone had brought these people the gospel plus cultural baggage.

Effective mission doesn't do that. It doesn't wrap Christianity up in extraneous issues which have nothing to do with the hearer of the message. Of course no-one can escape their own cultural ideas. We've all been shaped by the world view with which we've grown up. But the best witnesses spot what's intrinsic and what's extrinsic to the gospel, and don't off-load their accessories on those to whom they speak about Jesus.

Adding extras to Christianity causes real problems to many. I read today about a young Thai woman studying in the US who had just discovered she could be a Christian and also Thai. Until then she'd always believed she could be Thai and Buddhist, or Christian and no longer Thai in the sense of giving up everything from her own culture, including traits like meekness. She'd thought that accepting Christ had to mean abandoning her heritage. At last she'd seen she could follow Jesus in a Thai way, keeping things she'd learned from Buddhism about meekness and love and respect for her family. How sad, I reflected as I read her story, that anyone should think she couldn't be both Thai and Christian. How many still believe that? How many have we put off the gospel by adding our cultural trappings, making them think Christianity is, for example, the white man's or rich man's religion? And if it's that, it's not really for them.

Inviting people to become Christians is not inviting them to become like us. Those who are good at doing mission know that and don't require people to strip off what's legitimate in their existing way of life.

This isn't just to do with crossing national boundaries. This is an issue with evangelising next-door neighbours. The neighbour doesn't hear just an invitation to believe in Jesus. He hears that *plus* a requirement that he dresses up and goes to church on Sunday mornings. He doesn't want to do that. He wants to be in his bed catching up on sleep or reading his newspaper on a Sunday morning. Or, not only does he hear about Jesus but he hears that he should be at church meetings three evenings every week. He doesn't want that either. He'll lose his friends for they're in the pub or on the golf course. Or, as well as hearing about Jesus, he hears that he'll have to start reading a 1500-page book with tiny print and very hard to understand words. He'd rather read a magazine, or do a crossword. Maybe he'd rather not read at all but just watch TV.

Okay, maybe we don't tell people they need to do all these things, but somehow they think they do. And sometimes we just drop it all on them later, once they've signed up, and then we frighten them back out the door they've just come through.

It could so easily have been like that when lots of young people started attending our church. Those who'd been members for years had prayed for God to convert the younger generation and fill the church with them. It was a great prayer, and it began to get answered. But the young people didn't turn up with freshly scrubbed faces, neatly tied ties, sitting in straight rows in the pews, and rising on cue with hymn book in hand to sing the faithful songs of old to the stirring sound of the pipe organ. For one thing they tended to climb over the pews. For another they had a habit of sitting on the book rests when they were chatting to friends, and those book rests often couldn't take the strain and got broken. Then there were the tee-shirts. Instead of perfectly ironed formal shirts and ties, they arrived in decidedly unironed and gloriously extravagant tee-shirts. Some advertised their favourite brand of beer. Some had slogans crude enough to curl hair without a visit to the hairdresser. Then there was the music. They wanted songs with tempo, accompanied by lots of instruments including drums. And they wanted words in the songs that had lots of feeling. Sometimes they liked it if we threw out the order of service and just went with the flow of what was happening.

Those who had prayed for the young people to fill the church hadn't realised that when they did it would be like that. Without knowing it they'd imagined the incomers would just be younger, more energetic versions of themselves. When they weren't they could have tried to force them into their mould. Or they could have frowned the youngsters out of the church and reclaimed it for those who had been there first. But thankfully, they did neither of those. They're among the greatest saints I've ever known for they accepted those youngsters. It hurt to lose what they'd always had, but they valued what those youngsters gained even more. And many of them talked to them, and got to know them. Under the leather jackets, unshaven chins and long straggly hair (and that was just the girls) they found good people who had a passion for Jesus even if they would never have a passion for the old ways of the church.

Those who are good at mission don't say, 'Become a Christian like me.' They say, 'Become a Christian who will remain the unique person you are.' That's been fundamental since the early days of the Church. Back then there were some who wanted Gentile converts to start behaving like Jews. But the Church's leaders decided against it. Given the Jewish heritage of the first Christians it was a radical and brave decision, but a necessary one. As James recognised, 'we should not make it difficult for the Gentiles who are turning to God' (Acts 15:19). That decision was critical for the spread of the gospel.

Of course there are habits that must die and new ways that must be learned (next section!), but there's much that many of us dump on people which is only our baggage. No-one wants to carry unnecessary baggage. If we insist on it we'll win few to Jesus.

They call people to discipleship, not merely conversion

The Great Commission isn't to do with persuading people to believe the right things about Jesus. 'Therefore go and make disciples of all nations, baptising them in the name of the Father and of the Son and of the Holy Spirit, and teaching them to obey everything I have commanded you' (Matt. 28:19–20). The verb translated 'make disciples' is the Greek *mathēteuō*. Its base meaning has to do with becoming a pupil.

My first teacher was Miss McHardie. I was a five-year-old; she seemed ancient to me, which means she was over twenty-five. I owe her so much. I listened and learned from her: to read, to write, to count, and even to sing almost in tune. Miss McHardie was my guide into mysteries, my inspirer, my helper and more than once my disciplinarian. My life was shaped by her example, instruction and authority. That's what it meant for me to be her pupil, and that's the rock-bottom meaning here about converts and Jesus. He becomes their guide, their leader, their mentor, their ruler.

That's very different from someone going through a ritual of bowing his head, praying a prayer and thinking that he's done a transaction which guarantees him a place in heaven. And it's different from someone feeling a spiritual tingle run up his spine, sensing God's nearness, and in a single moment of emotional and spiritual passion promising to serve God for ever. Races aren't run because they're begun. Buildings aren't built because foundations are laid.

The temptation is to make entry into Christianity seem easy. Salesmen often mask the real price until the deal is clinched. That may work for marketing cars or insurance policies where there's no way out once someone's signed on the dotted line, but it's counterproductive when recruiting for Christ. For one thing people do walk away. They find Christianity doesn't generate permanent happiness and, in fact, some areas of life become tougher. It's not what they'd been led to believe, so they opt out. For another thing, even if they stay their influence is negative. They call themselves Christians but don't live for God. They're witnesses, but bad ones. They repel people from, rather than attracting them to, the faith.

Those who are good at mission make sure people are rightly born into the faith. They make sure people understand conversion is a beginning not an end. They make sure people know Jesus as Lord as well as Saviour. In other words they help create disciples for Jesus, people willing to submit every part of their lives to him, people who will go on to win others for him.

They don't abandon brand-new Christians

The greatest mixture of joy and terror which can be combined in one experience comes to first-time parents when they take their new-born home from hospital. This gift of God – complete with ten fingers, ten toes, two ears, two eyes, one mouth, and a waste-disposal system that seems programmed for a productivity bonus – is probably one of the most desired objects anyone can have. Yet even as you breathe a prayer of thanks, you scream a prayer for help. This baby doesn't feed itself or change itself. It doesn't choose its own clothes, set the temperature of its bath water, nor tell you why it's crying. It's fragile. It's dependent. If you fail, it can't help itself. Without you that baby can't survive. Your child needs you.

Similarly, new Christians need their spiritual 'parents' for longer than the moment of entry into the faith. Conversion does not infuse knowledge of God's will into the convert. That's why the Great Commission includes a command to teach those who have become disciples.

The goal is not dependency but maturity. It's giving someone the tools, the knowledge, the experience on which to build a faith that can withstand temptation, disaster, and assault. I once constructed a raft. It was highly unstable and liable to tip me off at any moment. It was fun to lark around with in the shallows, but I wouldn't have taken it into deep water. That would have been too risky with something so flimsy. Many have a faith that survives only in the shallows. When life pushes them out into the deep they drown. Those who are good at mission know that, and do all they can to help people build a strong faith, to be mature as Christians.

There are two major ways in which learning happens. One by what's taught and the other by what's caught. The first tends to be formal and programmed. The second is usually neither. The new Christian needs both.

There are dozens of instruction series on the basics of the faith. There isn't one that's better than all the rest because what works for Jill isn't what works for Jane. But some teaching programme is almost always useful. New believers simply won't get a systematic understanding of the faith by listening to sermons, and most haven't the ability to research for themselves. The discipline and orderliness of going through a programmed course is good. Many 'older' Christians wish they'd had one when they became Christians.

A course like that is half of what's needed. The other half is practical discipline. The formal learning programme can usually be taught by anyone with the right gift, but informal mentoring requires a relationship of honesty, trust and respect. That's hard to organise. Often the initiative will need to lie with mature Christians adopting newcomers. If they've helped them come to faith, the relationship is already there. If not, like all deep relationships it'll take time and mutual commitment to become strong. But it's a relationship that's sorely needed for the new Christian. Who can he or she ask all the questions that sound foolish in public? How long should I pray for? Is there a right posture for prayer? What do I say when I'm told that I just have blind faith? Can I go to a pub for a drink? Should I break off the relationship with my non-Christian girlfriend or boyfriend? How much of an offering should I give? Do I need to go to two services on a Sunday? Should I go to my friend's birthday party on Sunday evening though it means missing church? Can I go shopping with my Mum on Sunday? How do I reply to the fellow at work who says all the suffering in the world proves God is either not all powerful or not all caring? Can I wear jeans to church? Some of these questions seem trivial, but they're not to the new Christian. He or she needs someone to ask.

A discipling relationship isn't just about answering questions. It's also about modelling prayer, witness, Bible study, loving others, sacrifice and so on. It's showing how being a Christian impacts all areas of life. This is virtually a master and apprentice relationship. Ideally it's being able to use Paul's words, 'Follow my example, as I follow the example of Christ' (1 Cor. 11:1).

That's healthy. And it's the best of training for the young Christian. One day he or she will do the same for someone. The aim is to grow strong disciples.

When one of my daughters was about two she jumped into a swimming pool before anyone had put safety armbands on her. She expected to float, and there was a look of great distress and terror on her face as she gradually sank. Thankfully I was nearby for rescue. It's a myth to say people should be thrown into the deep end, whether literally in a swimming pool or metaphorically into all the demands and problems of being a Christian in a hostile and difficult world. For a time people need help. When the hard times come, the relationship with a more mature Christian will be one of the most crucial factors in helping the new Christian survive.

Mission doesn't end with conversion. Those who are good at it make sure the right blend of formal and informal learning is there so no-one sinks unnecessarily.

They rely on the Spirit, not on programmes or techniques

A drawing that taught me a lesson is of a man trying to make a hole in a wall with an electric drill which is not plugged into a socket. Of course it isn't working properly, so he's thumping the drill with a huge mallet. He gets a crude hole that way, but it's not satisfactory and it's far more effort than it need be.

Is that what my evangelism is like? Am I trying to make breakthroughs for the gospel by thumping obstacles hard? When the going gets tough, do I just summon up more of my strength and initiative and hit harder? If I rely on my evangelism techniques or skills from the witness training programme, maybe that's exactly what I do.

Fine words and fine methods achieve much, but neither generates spiritual life in anyone. Only God does that, and it's the work of his Spirit. Those who are good at mission have learned a sensitivity and dependency on the Spirit far more than they have mastered methods and techniques of witness.

People make two (almost) opposite mistakes. Some forget conversion is the Spirit's work. We want quick results, and so we latch on to any new thing that seems to offer a fast track to effective witnessing or church growth. I've got stacks of manuals and books on my shelves, the evidence of all the conferences I've attended or shops I've scoured looking for the secret. Often I've thought I've found it, brought the method back and tried it out. Sometimes it's seemed to work for a while, but then it loses its power. Like a recipe that produced a gourmet meal when used by the master chef but became a burnt offering in my hands, so my wonder method that should have produced daily conversions is proving as barren as every one of its predecessors. These days there are fewer of those books and manuals going on to my shelves, because there's no secret formula out there. The flyers will still come through the post tempting me to believe that only if I go to the next great conference will I find the way to do it, the way that takes away the grind and assures success. But it won't. The more I rely on any method the less I rely on God. And I must rely on him, for ultimately he's the only one who gives people new birth.

Others fall into a quite different trap. They think that no techniques matter. They'll simply let the natural overflow of the Spirit in them draw people to Jesus. God will use their cheerfulness, peacefulness and goodness. One day, when people ask what gives this quality of life, they'll be given the right words that will bring those enquirers to Christ. But all too often people never ask. Maybe they think this perpetually cheerful, peaceful and kind person is not quite real and they're suspicious. Maybe all they think is that he's a good person. Maybe if they do ask they're so confused by a muddled response they're not helped by the explanation and never ask again. Looking for opportunities to speak about Jesus, and knowing what to say when those opportunities come is not unspiritual. It's common sense and caring. Learning from an evangelism programme is not futile. Trusting in it to save people is what's futile.

Not everyone in the Bible who was a good evangelist had a great technique. Jonah was a disaster in presenting an attractive message. His words to Nineveh, 'Forty more days and Nineveh will be overturned' (Jonah 3:4), must rank as one of the most brutal and brief sermons ever delivered. But it also ranks as about the most effective. 'The Ninevites believed God. They declared a fast, and all of them, from the greatest to the least, put on sackcloth' (Jonah 3:5). Those who polish and perfect their sermons have every right to feel jealous that Jonah's grudged and imperfect message saw the conversion of a whole city.

But those who are good at mission know it's not the polishing and perfecting of their message that brings people to faith. Sure, we must offer our best to God, but it's his Spirit through our work and our words who helps needy people. He touches people through our hands. He speaks to people through our mouths.

Dixie was an important person for me when I was seventeen. She was my landlady during part of my first year in the big city. She'd never done a course on witness in her life. She broke every rule of subtlety in the way she spoke, and her humour didn't fit easily with the sense of propriety of some of the more stuffy church members. But she was a Christian with a great sense of fun, and a huge heart that made people feel valued. It was the first home I'd ever known where people didn't ring the doorbell but came straight in. And Dixie had time for them or, if she didn't, they made themselves coffee and she chatted to them while she got on with her work. I don't remember ever being witnessed to while I lived there. But Jesus seemed more real and becoming a Christian more important by the time I left. Within a year two of us who had lived there were converted.

There's no-one who's mastered everything about witness. But thankfully no-one has to graduate with a top honours degree in evangelism before God can use them. Getting hold of a few basic principles helps, and then getting on and doing it, knowing that conversion is God's work and he will bring people to faith, not us. There's no reason why every Christian can't be good at mission.

Chapter 9

A dream mission

THE STORY IS told of a man walking along a beach strewn with washed-up starfish. Thousands of the starfish lay stranded above the shoreline, certain to die before the tide returned later in the day. As the man made his way along the edge of the sea, he picked up a starfish here and there and flung it back into the waves.

Another figure strolling on the beach saw what he did and, as they met, said, 'Why do you bother? There are thousands of these starfish. What difference can you make?'

The first man looked at the starfish in his hand, threw it to safety in the sea, and answered, 'A lot of difference to that one.'

Mission makes that kind of difference. Mission matters because it changes lives. Never as many as we would wish, but at least some have their whole eternities changed.

It happened to John. He looked anything but a likely recruit for Christianity. His shoulder-length blond hair somehow contrasted yet belonged with his scruffy leather motorcycle jacket. Apart from riding his noisy and dirty machine, John's other passion was power-lifting. He had such a slight but strong frame he could beat almost anyone at straight lifts of enormous weights. His rough accent masked a powerful intellect and disarming honesty, primed by the insights he got from studying psychology. His friends were all types, from heroes to villains. His lifestyle didn't put him on the virtue side of the fence. His ego was far from underdeveloped, and he loved to be the centre of attention. Yet that trait was balanced by an immense generosity and concern for others. He frequently gave his last penny away to someone he reckoned needed it more. At age twenty-one, with no church background, belonging to a category of society that was least reachable with the gospel, John should never have given Christianity a first thought, never mind serious consideration.

But he did. John was befriended by Christians. He pushed them away, saying he wasn't interested. But he was. He had part-time work as a security guard. Late at night he read the Gideon's New Testament he'd been given as a child. Matthew's Gospel gripped him. The Jesus described there contrasted so strongly with what he thought Christianity was about. The reality of Jesus's life and message about God grabbed a mind that refused to deal in anything less than truth. 'God is God, and you can't get round that,' he eventually decided.

So he had to come to terms with that God. The message of Jesus dying in his place became real, and the challenge of living a new life for God gripped him. And he found Christians didn't reject him but valued and loved him. It wasn't instantaneous, but John was converted.

That changed him, but not everything about him. First time in church and he stood up at the end of my sermon and applauded. He said later, 'Go anywhere else and you applaud if someone does well.' He charmed the young ladies, probably to the terror of their mothers – though he charmed most of the mothers too. No-one could have been more willing to go on learning about the faith and get involved in doing things for God. When we had a major denominational event in our city, I asked John to help with stewarding. Having a young person from our church taking up the offering would impress the visiting delegates. It impressed them more than I meant, because John turned up wearing a tee-shirt with a graphic picture of a frustrated hedgehog trying to have sex with a scrubbing brush. There were parts of John's sanctification which took longer than others.

But it is happening. These days John is married to a lovely Christian girl. His employment is psychology, but he finds himself increasingly busy preaching at weekends. His penetrating intellect, ruthless honesty, deep insights and sharp communication skills are being used for God.

Mission works. Lives get changed. Heaven gets populated. Before they ever get there, God's people make this world a bit more like God always wanted it to be. His kingdom comes on earth as it exists already in heaven. Because his kingdom is first in us rather than around us, that's true no matter whether it's just one life affected or many. The dying thief on the cross never had time to 'witness' to others, but God came into his life. A child of God was born. Someone heading for a lost eternity became someone heading for heaven. Others have more time and opportunity to make a difference for people with their changed lives. They can be big influencers, like Billy Graham, John Bunyan, Martin Luther, William Carey, or Mother Teresa. Or they can be nearly unknown influencers, like a mother who saw her family as her calling. Her three sons became teachers and preachers of the gospel and they've made a difference in thousands of lives. They've been noticed by the public, but where would they have been without a mother who prayed for them, taught them the Bible, disciplined them to live rightly, and instilled a good sense of priorities?

Jesus's expectations

Mission changes lives and so changes the world. Some Christians know that and speak boldly and confidently about Jesus, expecting their families and friends to be changed. And often they are. But many westernised Christians seem to have stopped believing in mission. They've lost confidence. They go through the motions but don't really anticipate anyone coming to faith or their church growing. They consider ineffectiveness normal.

> Listen! A farmer went out to sow his seed. As he was scattering the seed, some fell along the path, and the birds came and ate it up. Some fell on rocky places, where it did not have much soil. It sprang up quickly, because the soil was shallow. But when the sun came up, the plants were scorched, and they withered because they had no root. Other seed fell among thorns, which grew up and choked the plants, so that they did not bear grain. Still other seed fell on good soil. It came up, grew and produced a crop, multiplying thirty, sixty, or even a hundred times.
>
> Mark 4:3–8

Jesus expected far greater results from mission than most

western Christians. One parable shows that clearly, the parable of the sower. This is Jesus's norm for mission. There are several key points.

Jesus expected definite efforts to do mission

Jesus expected mission to get done. He began, 'Listen! A farmer went out to sow his seed' (Mark 4:3). Of course he did. The farmer didn't think he'd get a harvest by reading books on agriculture, by studying soil structure or sowing techniques, nor from sitting back all through the season in front of a warm fire. He knew he had to get out of his armchair and into the field to sow seed.

When I was about fifteen, my brother Alan allowed me to tag along with him when he went to a huge dance hall on a Saturday evening. It gave an outing to my corduroy jacket, long pointed-collar shirt, knitted wool tie, drainpipe trousers and semi-platform shoes. Image was important. The dance hall was packed with people, a real maelstrom of noise, colour, heat and sound. All the young women were on the dance floor, and when the pop group played they danced with each other. Meanwhile the fellows stood in an immense circle round the dance floor and watched them, trying not to look interested but missing nothing and no-one. That first Saturday night Alan and I stood with the lads and we watched too. Next week we turned up, stood among the young men, and for the whole evening watched again. Third week we joined the big circle of fellows, and again we watched. But by now Alan and I were getting fed up with just being spectators. This was expensive entertainment. So, next time the group started playing, we nodded to each other, walked on to the dance floor, tapped two young ladies on the shoulder, and mouthed, 'Dance?' To our amazement they turned and danced with us. This was wonderful. Five minutes later we were dancing with two others, and on it went like that for the whole evening. Never again did we join the circle of spectators. We had learned the lesson. No asking, no dancing. Ask, and they danced with you.

No sowing, no reaping. Without effort, no harvest. The farmer knew that, so he got the seed into the soil. Jesus expected his word to be sown too. There'd be no harvest with it still in the store.

The first Christians certainly understood the 'no sowing, no

> The farmer sows the word. Some people are like seed along the path, where the word is sown. As soon as they hear it, Satan comes and takes away the word that was sown in them. Others, like seed sown on rocky places, hear the word and at once receive it with joy. But since they have no root, they last only a short time. When trouble or persecution comes because of the word, they quickly fall away. Still others, like seed sown among thorns, hear the word; but the worries of this life, the deceitfulness of wealth and the desires for other things come in and choke the word, making it unfruitful. Others, like seed sown on good soil, hear the word, accept it, and produce a crop – thirty, sixty or even a hundred times what was sown.
>
> MARK 4:14–20

reaping' principle. Every chance that came they spread the word about Jesus:

Acts 2 At Pentecost the Spirit falls, the disciples go into the streets praising God, a crowd gathers, Peter preaches to them and thousands are converted.

Acts 3 A lame man is healed at the entrance to the temple, another crowd gathers, and Peter and John preach, and talk to them about Jesus.

Acts 4 Evangelism has got Peter and John into trouble, they're dragged before the Sanhedrin to be warned about their behaviour, but they use the opportunity to witness some more about Jesus.

Acts 5 All the apostles get arrested, but they're miraculously freed during the night and start teaching the gospel again in the temple courts.

Acts 6 and 7 Stephen witnesses boldly, gets arrested on trumped-up charges, but keeps on declaring the good news right until his death.

Acts 8 Persecution in Jerusalem spreads the disciples to other places, including Samaria where Philip preaches and sees great numbers coming to faith.

Acts 9 Paul gets converted, immediately starts to witness about Jesus, and soon begins a whole new phase of deliberate, planned mission.

On and on the story goes. These Christians didn't think it enough that they had come to faith, nor did they think mission would simply happen by itself. They took opportunities and planned definite actions so that the word of God spread.

Mission is no accidental or automatic activity. The seed has to be taken out of the sack and thrown in the soil.

Jesus accepted that some harvest would be lost
Jesus described three situations in which the sowing would prove fruitless:

- Some seed would fall on the path, and get snatched away by birds – like Satan stealing the word before it could take root.
- Some would land on rocky ground where there was no depth for it to get established – like those who melt away in the face of persecution.
- Some would be sown among thorns which would choke the seed – like those for whom the temptations and pressures of 'things' would kill the word in them.

Not all the sown seed would produce a harvest. Not all would last. The farmer would have losses.

If ever there was realism about mission, this is it. No matter how fine the seed or how clever the sowing – how good the evangelistic content or presentation – there are still many who won't believe. Some suggest that if only we did things their way and had enough faith we'd see people everywhere flocking into churches. Jesus never taught that. Nor was it his experience. No-one has ever had purer content to his message. No-one has had a life more filled with the Spirit. No-one has ever done more astounding miracles. Yet no-one has ever been more rejected than Jesus.

In this parable Jesus was warning his disciples to expect failure with some. There would be people who would turn their backs on the good news.

But rejection hurts. It hurts in the same way that offering a gift and having it refused hurts. We've meant kindness, and it's been spurned. Rejection hurts also as a doctor is saddened when his best advice is rejected, knowing that the patient is choosing a lifestyle that will lead to ill health and maybe death.

I made a pastoral evangelism visit to a couple who received me politely, allowed me to explain the gospel, but then made it clear they'd rather I didn't come back. They didn't want to become Christians. I accepted what they said, told them I'd return any time if they wanted to hear more, and left. As I closed their gate and walked down the street, I cried. I knew what their decision meant for them. It distressed me to think they could be so definite that they didn't want to know Jesus.

Of course, most are not that articulate about refusing to believe, but their indifference is obvious. Many don't hear and then reject; they don't even want to hear. Christianity is irrelevant. They don't imagine there could be anything about it for them. It feels like the seed perishes the second it hits the ground.

When we meet rejection or apathy over and over again it depresses the spirit and dampens motivation. After a while we stop trying. Rather than make a great effort with high hopes only to have it all come to nothing, we reckon we know in advance what the outcome will be. If the seed is bound to be lost, why sow it? That's where many individuals and churches have reached.

Discouragement is a powerful force, and a serious cancer in the western church today. 'I tried sharing my faith with my colleague, and he just laughed. I won't be doing that again.' 'We ran an evangelistic event ten years ago, didn't add a single person to the church, so we won't be trying another.'

It's easy to condemn statements like these. We laugh and cry at the 'tried it once – didn't work' mentality that dogs church life. But it's born of long-term disappointment. Not trying has become a coping mechanism to avoid the pain of failure. If my brother and I had walked on to the dance floor, asked a couple of girls to dance with us and been turned down, that would have been humiliating.

We might have tried again and been refused again. If that had happened a few more times, we'd eventually have lost all self-confidence, hidden in the safe circle of the watchers, and wouldn't have dared try any more. Probably no amount of nagging or encouragement would have budged us. We'd have resisted that pressure more easily than we could have coped with the embarrassment and hurt of further rejection.

There are three antidotes to this discouragement about mission.

One is knowing that some failure is normal. That's what Jesus is teaching here. People have choices, and they won't all make the choice we want. That isn't necessarily failure on our part, any more than Adam's and Eve's decision to eat the forbidden fruit was failure by God. There will always be those who reject, and we need to be tough enough to cope with that.

Two is knowing that some rejections aren't final. A few weeks after my wife Alison was converted, she wrote to the man who'd taught her years before in Bible class to tell him that Jesus had become real for her. Back came a reply filled with gratitude for the news. He'd taught lots of teenagers, most of whom didn't seem to pay much attention. Often he'd wondered if the work had been worth it. It had. The seed had taken root secretly with at least one of those all too easily distracted youngsters, though if Alison hadn't written he'd never have known it had come to harvest. My guess is that there are many like that, and probably only in heaven will we ever know the full effect our witness has had.

Three is an attitude that refuses to give up. One time when I was speaking about discouragement, I asked the congregation, 'How many of you, when you were younger, learned to ride a bicycle?' Virtually every hand went up. Then I asked, 'How many of you, while you were learning, fell off?' Almost the same number of hands shot up again. They smiled. I hardly needed to make my point. It's common to struggle and even to fail for a time. Sometimes we get hurt in the process. (Only those who never try anything avoid all failure and all pain, but they rust out doing nothing.) Giving up, though, isn't the answer. Getting up and going forward often means success comes eventually.

With mission, losses happen. We wish they didn't. If we're wise, we'll check to see if there's anything that could have been done to prevent them. But we won't give up. We'll try again.

Jesus expected a great harvest
This parable has three negatives of failed seed sowing. It's said that just one negative outweighs any number of positives. So it's not surprising that three have obliterated from many people's attention the overwhelming positive of what happens from the sowing of good seed. 'Others, like seed sown on good soil, hear the word, accept it, and produce a crop – thirty, sixty or even a hundred times what was sown' (Mark 4:20).

By anyone's standard in any age that's a superb harvest. It's Jesus's expectation from good seed. Where his word takes proper root in people's lives, where they become his disciples, the harvest from them will be thirty, sixty or even a hundred times. That's an immense rate of reproduction. That's a fantastic effectiveness in mission from every Christian.

Mission is meant to work. The Church is meant to grow. In vast chunks of the world it is growing. There's astonishing growth these days in parts of Africa, Asia and South America, about 53,000 new Christians every day in the world.

Jesus expected that, and more. He told Peter and the other apostles, 'I will build my church, and the gates of Hades will not overcome it' (Matt. 16:18). There is immense determination and certainty in those words. This will happen. Jesus's Church will be strong, secure and, in the best sense, powerful. It will achieve what he wants, and nothing will thwart it.

It was the end of the violin lesson for my class, and David and I had the task of moving the piano back to the end of the school hall. It was a heavy piano to get moving though ran easily on its castors once started. We heaved and tugged with all the strength that two twelve-year-olds could manage. As we pushed it up the hall, one of us joked what a great battering ram the piano would make. The words hung in the air . . . A glint appeared in our eyes. Virtually without another word, we surveyed the huge oak door at the far end of the hall. It was immense. Our school had once been a castle, and this door was as solid as they came. We pulled the piano into position, got our shoulders behind it, shoved hard to get it rolling in the right direction and then let go. It stopped halfway. We dragged it back so we could have more distance to get up to speed. This time we pushed really hard. The piano started moving faster than any piano had ever moved up that hall. We got up to running speed, kept it on line until it was only three metres from the door, then released it. Straight into the middle of the door it went. There was an immense twang of strings and a crack of wood. The door stood unmoved. The piano fell apart.

That door was more powerful than a heavyweight piano. The door resisted the force that came against it. Jesus's teaching is that that will *not* be how it is as his Church goes forward. He is building his Church – adding to his disciples – and nothing, no human opposition and not even the gates of the underworld, will overcome it. No power of evil will stand against his Church. Darkness will not consume light.

That could be empty triumphalism. It's not. Jesus never pretended his people would march forward untroubled or unhurt. The Church's advance will be with successes *and* failures, not sweeping all before. It will be with hard work, with no special formulas for success. There will be casualties, for sacrifice and death are normal Christianity. But it *will* happen. Mission will be done. Jesus's Church will be built.

How sad that people grow used to smallness or ineffectiveness. When the church to which I belonged first saw a number of people becoming Christians one after the other within a short space of time, the question some asked was 'I wonder when it will stop?' When the church of which I was pastor debated whether to move to a larger building to give space for the increased numbers attending, some said, 'But when we get small again, it'll be too large a building for us.' I said, 'Why must growth stop? Why would we ever be small again?' Jesus expected his Church to move forward and keep moving. Mission will be effective. We've got so used to decline and disappointment we think it *normal*. It's not normal; it's Jesus's *abnormal*.

Changed priorities

If we're ever to see Jesus's norm come to pass, there will have to be effort, sacrifice and a new set of priorities. And those new priorities can reach the top of our agendas only if we evict other things.

Over the years I've seen what preoccupies all too many Christians and dominates church meetings, and it's not mission.

My first ever deacons' meeting had the 'offering bags versus offering plates' debate. Someone was willing to make a gift to the church of bags to replace the wooden plates the church was using. Presumably the donor wanted privacy for offerings. Debate raged to and fro on such an exciting topic, but the gift was eventually rejected on the grounds that if no-one could see what people were giving then offerings would decline. We kept the plates.

This was a mere foretaste of equally vital issues to come. The greatest anger I've ever seen in a meeting had to do with the Haas effect. I'm still not too sure what it is – clarity of explanation was not paramount in the middle of the argument – but it has something to do with the fact that sound from a loudspeaker reaches a hearer at a fractionally different moment from the natural sound of the (live) speaker's voice. If one is significantly nearer the hearer than the other then the gap in time between hearing from the two sources, the Haas effect, can cause the sound to be muffled. Hence it's important to place the loudspeakers wisely to minimise the problem. Two of my deacons couldn't agree on where those loudspeakers should be. To and fro strong words raged, with me refereeing lamely in the middle. Finally, because they were really friends and just hiding it well for the argument, they calmed down and we reached an acceptable solution. But it wasn't fun.

Nor was it fun after our church opened its own building and plans were being made for the Christmas party. Was it acceptable for people to wear black-soled shoes? 'They'll leave scuff marks on our brand-new floor, so they'll have to change into trainers when they arrive,' one said. 'You can't ask grown people to change their shoes like little children,' another pleaded. 'Are you going to scrub the black marks from the floor?' came the reply. In the end, and the end was a long time coming, we compromised that we would ask people to be careful and try not to leave marks on the floor.

These things are not unusual. Should we buy china plates or will paper ones do? Can the youth club play with a ball in the church hall? Does the crèche need new toys? The other day I asked some people what had taken up lots of time at their church meetings. Here are a few of their examples:

- 'Should we have a real or artificial Christmas tree in the sanctuary? And what size should it be?'
- 'What should be on the menu of the harvest supper?'
- 'Should there be a rubber or tin lid on the church refuse can? And should we write the name of the church in white paint on the lid?'
- 'What colour should we paint the wall? And will the finished shade on plaster be the same as the samples we're looking at which are painted on wood?'
- 'What can we do with the out-of-tune and past-its-best piano donated in memory of Constance Herkins, who died sixty years ago but whose grandson still comes to the church?'

My favourite is one of the simplest:

- 'Can we move the piano from the left side of the sanctuary to the right side?'

I bet that one ran for a long time.

If the dream of effective mission is ever to become a reality, we've got to stop indulging ourselves with these debates. They're a luxury a dying world can't afford to give us. The positioning of loudspeakers, or the menu for the harvest supper and even where the piano is placed all matter. But they don't matter so much that a whole church should be taken up with debating them, and they don't matter more than putting the gospel before a lost world. If we generated as much enthusiasm for mission as we do for issues which really don't have eternal significance, many churches which are going backward would be going forward.

A mission dream

I have a mission dream.

I dream of Christians sharing their faith enthusiastically, fearing God more than they fear anyone else, willing to sacrifice their comfort and even their lives so others can have the gospel.

I dream of Christians caring for people others reject, being first in places of need and still being there when others have left, and loving people even though the cost is losing out yourself.

I dream of Christians standing for what's right, for truth, for justice, defending the powerless and speaking for the voiceless, and not letting others set the agenda of society and the world.

I dream of Christians changing the world, standing against evil and initiating what's good, winning respect and trust even from those who don't share their faith.

I dream, in other words, of God's people leading the world, of Christians as the most effective force globally, not in some world-wide political movement to dominate others but as those who will put first the good of all people, not the selfish comfort and advantage of the few.

I believe that dream should have the chance to be reality. I see nothing in the character or power of God which makes it impossible. There's plenty in the weakness and frailty of humanity that could wreck it, but there's nothing inevitable about failure. Far from it. If darkness will never overcome the light, then there's no-one for whom Christian faith is impossible, no institution or thought system that can't be transformed, and no social problem so great it can't be resolved. If all of that is true, then everyone ought to have the opportunity of faith, every anti-Christian force ought to be challenged, and every troubled part of the world flooded with God's love through caring people.

I read old missionary biographies, and find myself deeply moved by them. There are tales there of great hardship, immense heroism and incredible commitment. I don't idealise these missionaries of a former era – some of them were probably very difficult to live with. Yet as I read of their hopes, their sacrifices, their dedication and their determination I wonder how we compare today. Do we have the depth and strength of vision they had for giving the gospel to the world? Will we take on impossible odds believing that with God all things are possible? Are we ready to lay down our lives so others can live?

The final challenge
Do any of us today really believe in mission? Do we really believe people who don't know of Christ are lost? Do we really believe

evangelising, caring, working for a better world are God's priorities for the lives of his children?

The answers to these questions don't lie in our official theological position, nor in our tally of evangelistic courses attended. What we really believe about anything is shown by what we do.

Years ago I played rugby for a team called Cambuslang Athletic. The name was a bit of a misnomer, because most of us didn't come from Cambuslang and none of us were athletic. The Third Fifteen for whom I played excelled only in consistency: we always lost. We did it in style, on average by a margin of about fifty points. None of us ever turned up for training, and usually a few didn't turn up for the match, so losing was inevitable.

Only once was it different. Once a miracle happened, though it was a miracle with a rational explanation. The First team game had been called off, and with several of our players not turning up we drafted some of the First Fifteen into our Third Fifteen and didn't tell the opposition. Come half time that day we weren't losing. The scores were something like twelve each. As we stood in a circle, gasping for air during our short respite, a strange look came over the faces of those of us who were regular losers. We might win! The thought had never occurred to us before. We were totally programmed to lose, and since we were normally down by some twenty or thirty points by half time we never went into the second period with any enthusiasm. We'd just crawl our way through the rest of the match, trying to keep out of trouble. But, as we gazed around the circle that half time, the thought that we could win swept over us. Suddenly, from somewhere deep inside, inspiration, motivation and determination rose. Adrenaline flowed. Energy coursed through our veins. The idea of victory gripped us. We went into that second half running, tackling, kicking and scratching like we had never done before on a rugby field. And we won! Only once, but we won. We believed it could happen, so we worked to make it happen.

What we really believe is shown by what we do. What, then, do our lives say we really believe about mission?

My heavenly Father is a missionary God. He loves the world as much as he ever did, and his heart beats with compassion for those still lost to him. His Spirit roams to and fro searching for all his children, never resting until every one is found.

I am that Father's child. His nature of love for the lost is in me. Believing in mission is utterly inevitable and totally natural. I could not be God's child and be otherwise.

I am part of a large family. If that family will stand together, honour their Father and do his work as their highest priority, then the unbelief and evil which is everywhere can be changed. The Father's love hasn't waned. Jesus's commission still applies. The Spirit's power is on us. Why shouldn't people everywhere come to faith? Why shouldn't God's touch be felt? Why shouldn't God's kingdom come on earth?

I believe in mission.

Epilogue:
The Race

IT IS MIDNIGHT, but I am in the perpetual daytime of a busy hospital. I wait outside an operating theatre. The door opens, and a surgeon emerges and hands me a box. He speaks quickly: 'Our patient has died, but his heart can be used for transplant. A man 500 miles away will live if you can deliver this to his hospital by 7 a.m.'

I take the box, scan the address where it's needed, then hurry through the maze of corridors, and reach my van parked outside. I speed away, wheels spinning, gears crashing. I care little. Getting there on time is what matters.

I can almost feel the adrenaline pumping inside my head, yet it must battle with a weary desperation that this journey is doomed to failure. How can I make it? Drive 500 miles that night? Don't they know how tired I am? Don't they realise I've had no break for weeks? Is this really worth it? Does it matter?

Out of town I race, and on to the main road south. Past one car, then another I sweep, pushing the accelerator ever more firmly to the floor. I'm taking chances, but I'll never get there in time if I play for safety. Lights change from green to red, but I hurry through. Speed limit signs whiz past – I choose not to notice what they say.

The speedometer needle dances crazily as I accelerate, brake, accelerate and brake. The counter moves relentlessly round, clicking off the miles. But it's still too slow.

The stream of oncoming car lights hypnotise, pulling a blanket of heaviness over my fatigued eyes. I screw them tight, then open them wide, forcing my eyes to focus on the road. 'Stay awake,' I tell myself. 'Concentrate.'

The lights of unknown towns drift past my van. On and on I

press, the box on the floor beside me the constant reminder that there is a job to do. Minutes become hours, a few miles turn into many. Still my foot presses the accelerator. Still I stare at the road, determined to get there in time.

It's 3 a.m. Nearly half my time is gone and I've done little more than 200 miles. It's useless. I can never do it. 'Perhaps it doesn't matter,' I tell myself. 'Perhaps the patient is already dead, or maybe he wouldn't make it through the operation anyway.'

Up ahead I see a sign. 'Roadside services'. 'A rest . . . some coffee . . . some food . . .' Deep desire for a break from driving grips my tired mind. My foot lifts from the accelerator. 'I need to stop, I'm entitled to,' I tell myself. The van drifts towards the slip road as I let the speed fall away. I pull into the car park, slowing, thinking how good it will be to relax, perhaps to lie back and sleep . . .

But before the wheels have stopped turning, suddenly I feel my foot press hard again on the pedal, and my hands turn the wheel towards the exit road. In a moment I'm back on the highway, accelerating, driving harder than ever. A new, stronger thought has taken charge. 'You must get there. You can rest later. For now, a man's life depends on you getting a new heart to him.'

So on I drive, refreshed by determination and the sense of purpose. It's still hard. It still hurts to concentrate. But I have to do it.

5 a.m. – 130 miles to go. It rains, and I have to slow. Muscles tense, my head throbs, my bones ache. 6 a.m. – still 70 miles. On and on I drive, but I won't make it. In my head I hear the words, 'You were too long. He's dead.' 6.30 – the rain stops. Still 30 miles. How can I get through the maze of streets and the early-morning traffic to the hospital?

6.45 – a police car on the outskirts of town. The officers signal me to follow them. Traffic melts away in front of their blue flashing light. This way, that, at only two speeds, fast and faster. But how can it ever be quick enough? Ahead I see the towering buildings of the hospital. In my mind hope is engaged in a deadly battle with fear. Can this possibly be worth it?

We scream round the final corner, pull into the emergency bay, and jerk to a halt. I glance at my watch . . . The minute hand is just coming up to 7 a.m. I sag exhausted over the steering wheel, the door is pulled open and safe hands whisk the box from the floor and hurry it off to an operating room.

Hours later I learn the patient is alive. 'If you hadn't come when you did, he wouldn't have made it,' I'm told. I feel awed. To have brought someone the means of life: part of me hates the responsibility; part of me soars with exhilaration at the privilege. For at least this one man, my work has mattered.

Useful books

A Task Unfinished, Michael Griffiths, Monarch Publications (1996).

Evangelism for a New Age, John Drane, Marshall Pickering (1994).

Evangelism: Now and Then, Michael Green, Inter-Varsity Press (1979).

How to Give Away Your Faith, Paul Little, Inter-Varsity Press (2nd edn, 1988).

I Believe in Evangelism, David Watson, Hodder and Stoughton (1976).

Mission and Meaninglessness, Peter Cotterell, SPCK (1990).

Springboard for Faith, Alister McGrath and Michael Green, Hodder and Stoughton (1993).

The Faith of the Unbeliever, Martin Robinson, Monarch Publications (1994).

Tinker, Tailor, Missionary?, Michael Griffiths, Inter-Varsity Press and OM Publishing (1992).

Transforming Mission, David J. Bosch, Orbis Books (1991).

Mission agencies

There are hundreds of agencies for mission. This list covers only some of those based in Britain, but almost all agencies believe their task is to help people find God's call on their life, not merely to recruit for their own ranks. Therefore they willingly direct people to other agencies if they would be more appropriate.

Action Partners
Bawtry Hall
Bawtry
DONCASTER
DN10 6JH
Tel: 01302 710750

Africa Inland Mission
2 Vorley Road
LONDON
N19 5HE
Tel: 0171 281 1184

Baptist Missionary Society
PO Box 49
Baptist House
129 Broadway
DIDCOT
OX11 8XA
Tel: 01235 512077

Christian Literature Crusade
51 The Dean
ALRESFORD
SO24 9BJ
Tel: 01962 735281

Church Mission Society
Partnership House
157 Waterloo Road
LONDON
SE1 8UU
Tel: 0171 928 8681

FEBA Radio
Ivy Arch Road
WORTHING
BN14 8BX
Tel: 01903 237281

INTERSERVE
325 Kennington Road
LONDON
SE11 4QH
Tel: 0171 735 8227

INTERSERVE (Scotland)
12 Elm Avenue
Lenzie
GLASGOW
G66 4HJ
Tel: 0141 776 2943

Latin Link
38 Kennington Park Road
LONDON
SE11 4RS
Tel: 0171 582 4952

The Leprosy Mission
England and Wales Office
Goldhay Way
Orton Goldhay
PETERBOROUGH
PE2 5GZ
Tel: 01733 370505

Mission Aviation Fellowship
Ingles Manor
Castle Hill Avenue
FOLKESTONE
CT20 2TN
Tel: 01303 850950

Oasis Trust
87 Blackfriars Road
LONDON
SE1 8HA
Tel: 0171 928 9422

OMF International (UK)
Belmont
The Vine
SEVENOAKS
TN13 3TZ
Tel: 01732 450747

Operation Mobilisation
The Quinta
Weston Rhyn
OSWESTRY
SY10 7LT
Tel: 01691 773388

Salvation Army
PO Box 249
101 Queen Street
LONDON
EC4P 4EP
Tel: 0171 236 5222

SIM UK (Society for
International Ministries)
Joint Mission Centre
Ullswater Crescent
CROYDON
CR5 2HR
Tel: 0181 660 7778

Tear Fund
100 Church Road
TEDDINGTON
TW11 8QE
Tel: 0181 977 9144

Wycliffe Bible Translators
Horsleys Green
HIGH WYCOMBE
HP14 3XL
Tel: 01494 482521

WEC International
Bulstrode
Oxford Road
GERRARDS CROSS
SL9 8SZ
Tel: 01753 884631

Youth with a Mission
Highfield Oval
Ambrose Lane
HARPENDEN
AL5 4BX
Tel: 01582 765481

Below are listed two bodies that help mission agencies share information, consider issues of mutual interest and build cooperative strategies. They are useful points of contact about mission, and can help direct enquirers to specific agencies.

Churches Commission on
Mission
Inter-Church House
35 Lower Marsh
LONDON
SE1 7RL
Tel: 0171 620 4444

Evangelical Missionary Alliance
Whitefield House
186 Kennington Park Road
LONDON
SE11 4BT
Tel: 0171 735 0421

Information like this, plus the addresses of many other evangelistic and mission agencies, can be found in the *UK Christian Handbook*, available from bookshops and from Christian Research, Vision Building, 4 Footscray Road, Eltham, London SE9 2TZ. Tel: 0181 294 1989.